# The Quality Paradigm

## Why you and your business need it to succeed

# CHRISTOPHER GERGEN

authorHOUSE®

*AuthorHouse™*
*1663 Liberty Drive*
*Bloomington, IN 47403*
*www.authorhouse.com*
*Phone: 1-800-839-8640*

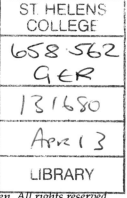
*No part of this book may be reproduced, stored in a retrieval system, or transmitted by any means without the written permission of the author.*

*First published by AuthorHouse 11/9/2010*

*ISBN: 978-1-4520-8910-2 (e)*
*ISBN: 978-1-4520-8912-6 (sc)*
*ISBN: 978-1-4520-8913-3 (hc)*

*Library of Congress Control Number: 2010914967*
*Gergen, Christopher Paul*
*The quality paradigm: why you and your business*
*need it to succeed / Christopher Gergen*

*1. Business    2. Management    3. Self-Help*
*Cover Designed by Joe French*
*Author Photograph © Katie Ward www.millerwardphotography.com*
*Editing by Brianne Sharpe*

*Printed in the United States of America*

*This book is printed on acid-free paper.*

*10   9   8   7   6   5   4   3   2   1   0*

*Because of the dynamic nature of the Internet, any Web addresses or links contained in this book may have changed since publication and may no longer be valid. The views expressed in this work are solely those of the author and do not necessarily reflect the views of the publisher, and the publisher hereby disclaims any responsibility for them.*

"It is not the critic who counts; not the man who points out how the strong man stumbles, or where the doer of deeds could have done them better. The credit belongs to the man who is actually in the arena, whose face is marred by dust and sweat and blood, who strives valiantly; who errs and comes short again and again; because there is not effort without error and shortcomings; but who does actually strive to do the deed; who knows the great enthusiasm, the great devotion, who spends himself in a worthy cause, who at the best knows in the end the triumph of high achievement and who at the worst, if he fails, at least he fails while daring greatly. So that his place shall never be with those cold and timid souls who know neither victory nor defeat."

President Theodore Roosevelt – 23 April 1910 – Paris, France

# DEDICATION

For my two beautiful daughters, Israel and Morgan.

I love you both more than words can express. Both of you serve to be the inspiration for everything I have accomplished in the past 15 years. Thank you for allowing me to be your "Daddy" and not just your father. Being your Daddy has been and always will be my greatest joy, my greatest accomplishment and my greatest pleasure.

My heart is forever yours.

Remember, little girls, no matter what you face today:

*"Easy-day."*

# ACKNOWLEDGEMENTS

I would like to begin by thanking all of my critics over the last 20 years. Today, I would not be the man that I am had it not been for each of you. I could not have asked for better gifts to enable my success. My heartfelt thanks go out to you all.

A huge thank you does not seem sufficient for my editor, Brianne Sharpe who spent many days and nights working through all of this material. Her patience and wonderful suggestions helped to make this book what I envisioned it to be. In addition, thank you to all of the proofreaders who looked at this manuscript repeatedly and helped me to clarify my message. I would also like to acknowledge my friends Joe French and Hans Gray who helped to create on screen what I was seeing in my head. Your creative gene and wonderfully patient demeanor put me at ease when I was worried about the presentation of this book.

Thank you to all of the professionals at AuthorHouse Publishing for helping to bring this message to the market.

Finally, I would like to thank my family for suffering through the lean and the hard times while I was learning these lessons. Thank you for allowing me to disappear into the bedroom to write or wonder off to a late night diner or a quiet café to read and research at all hours of the night. Thank you for being patient when I screwed things up and for celebrating with me when I got it right. Most of all, thank you for not giving up on me as so many others did over the years.

# CONTENTS

# INTRODUCTION

*We judge ourselves by what we feel capable of doing while others judge us by what we have already done.*

- Longfellow

I can only assume some of you are looking for the secret to success in life and in business, so here is the secret in the second sentence of this book.

The secret to success is *there is no secret.*

There is no shortcut, no silver bullet that you can utilize to become successful at anything or everything. Success takes the investment of time, energy, tears, struggles, good decisions, bad decisions and a hell of a lot of persistence when things seem like they are all falling apart. Success requires responsibility, accountability, and ownership when projects and plans fail to go as planned – because business rarely goes as planned. Success requires that you take control of your life, your business, and your relationships. There is no secret to success except *your* personal effort and good decisions. Success is something earned and never bestowed. You may inherit the consequences of success (or failure for that matter), but the success itself belongs to the person who earned it. An Irish proverb illustrates this point clearly: *"You have to do your own growin', no matter how tall your grandfather is."* The old truth remains that the only place "success" comes before "work" is in the dictionary. In the real world, success is never a given; you have to earn it every step of the way. There are no free lunches.

I wish I could tell you that the only requirement to overcoming your challenges in business and life is a read-through of this book. What wonderful magic that would be, if it were possible. Not to mention, I would probably sell a lot more of these books! Alas, the truth is more sobering. Most of the purchasers of this book will not read past the first chapter. Even less will read past the midway point in Chapter 6, and fewer still will finish the entire body of information. That is not the sobering part. The sobering part is even fewer – only a fraction – of everyone who reads this book will put *any* of the suggestions to work. The principles of the Quality Paradigm only work when they are used. Leadership and management philosophies only work with proper implementation followed by competent execution on a *continual basis*. Quality is not an event your company can host or a seminar you can attend so that the next day all aspects and areas of your business or your life are full of quality outputs and quality decisions. Quality is not a rainstorm that blows through and waters the ground in a single event. Quality is a process akin to a river that flows through dry valley places and gives life to the immediate surrounding areas. The Quality Paradigm is an eternal flame that will light the pathway for generation upon generation.

If I could reduce the concept of the Quality Paradigm down to one single idea, it would be to leave everything and everyone one, whenever possible, in a better condition or position than how you found them. I have always told my children since they were toddlers to leave things better than they found them. In fact, this was the first life lesson I ever taught to them, and it will be the last lesson that I teach to them before I die. When we go out to eat, I tell them to leave things better than they found them or at least in a condition that is easily cleaned. When we travel and stay in hotels, I tell them to strip the beds and pile the towels for ease of cleaning and to gather all of the trash after wiping the counters off. When we stay with family or friends, we clean the bathrooms we have used and strip the beds for them and offer to wash the sheets and towels we used. When my daughters come across someone who is in distress, they know to offer to help them if possible or to find someone in a position to provide assistance. When they undergo any task, they know they are to think about everything that needs to be accomplished and to consider whether their task will affect other people or events that will come behind them. This thinking process is routine for them because I consistently hold them to that standard.

These fundamentals of living a responsible life are also the fundamentals of being a responsible parent, businessperson, manager, leader, politician, or other authority figure. The genesis of effective leadership finds itself in first developing the Quality Paradigm. Whenever possible, leave everything and everyone better than you found them. Anyone who shows potential and interest in leadership and management can undergo training to learn how to lead and manage. However, even after learning the skills of leadership and management, many people hobble themselves with problems directly relating to their lack of being quality-conscience in their personal and professional conduct. Ethics and moral responsibility fit into the Quality Paradigm like a hand into a glove. The principles of general moral goodness (honesty, compassion for the weak, courage, etc.), competency, and work ethic comprise the idea of the Quality Paradigm.

## PERSPECTIVE

At the age of 16, I began to be interested in becoming the best person I could possibly become. From an even earlier age, I began to be conscious of the idea that my life was a gift that I intended to share with other people in a way that was meaningful and life changing for them. Much of my childhood experiences were just like many of yours. My experiences forced me to deal with depression, rejection, and difficult family dynamics. These difficulties and challenges shaped my focus in life and ultimately determined my deep desire to help others. I was not conscious of some magical destiny in the sense that I believed some eternal being or cosmic force chose me out of the masses to be a great leader (which I do not believe I am). Rather, I simply had a sense of desire for personal greatness and a fire inside that yearned to keep moving forward despite life's obstacles.

It was not until years later that I began to understand that people do not have preset destinies. The destination at the end of your life is hand crafted by the worker who stares back at you every morning in the mirror. You are the artisan who creates the masterpiece that is to be your life. The decisions you made in all of your yesterdays have determined where you are right here in the present. Even if you have been victimized in some way or have experienced unforeseen and horrific events in your life, there is a space of time, often less than a second, between the event and your reaction to those events where you have the ultimate power in the universe: the power of choice. I say that choice is the ultimate power in the universe because all things in the physical universe operate based on cause and effect. This is not so with the human experience. As humans, we have the power of choice when "causes" appear. Most times, we cannot choose the events that happen to us, but we do retain the power to choose the affect of the effect of these events in our lives. After all, sometimes "shit happens" for no reason. The world is random in many ways, and you must learn to dance and sway with the tempo of life. There is no cosmic supernatural force picking on you. There is no cosmic supernatural force making opportunity for you while screwing somebody else in the process. The bottom line is "shit happens" to all of us, and in that small fraction of a moment in time between what happens to us and how we react, we choose what meaning we are going to allow it to have in our lives (if any at all).

You assign the meaning and response that will drive your behavior and ultimately your destination at the end of your life. You choose what type of life you will live. You choose what becomes of your life. You choose how to view events in your life and influences you allow to shape your thinking. The Quality Paradigm begins and ends with you and with your choices that drive your behaviors. Your behaviors ultimately determine your experiences whether intended or unintended. Your life is the consequence of your close embrace of the Quality Paradigm or your wholesale dismissal of it.

## THE QUALITY PARADIGM IN ACTION

Over the years, I have had the distinct opportunity to work with many dedicated and dynamic leaders and managers. I could literally fill a book with examples of people displaying the Quality Paradigm in their everyday lives. Below are the brief stories of two outstanding people with whom I have had the opportunity to work. Many of the most valuable lessons I have internalized into my own thinking and habits have come from people just like the two people I highlight below in the following paragraphs.

*Story 1:*

There is a young woman I have known for a little over a year that has so impressed me with how strongly she possesses the Quality Paradigm that her story is worth sharing with you here. I hope that her story will serve as an encouragement to those of you who may be facing tough challenges and considering allowing those challenges to offer excuse for not performing to your highest potential. Upon our first introduction, Erin Martin was a new hire at a quickly growing internet-based business. At first glance, she seemed like any other young woman getting started in business and in life. She was a college graduate and worked in the service industry off and on most of her adult life. She does not have an Ivy League education or a long list of letters behind her name. Her family is not wealthy. There was nothing particularly extraordinary in the way of work experience on her resume'. What immediately separated Erin from many of her peers was her dynamic affinity for old-fashioned work. In an age where cutting corners and general laziness is often recast as "working smarter," she applied her skills of organization, a relentless work ethic, and the Quality Paradigm to set herself up for success.

For the first three months of working with Erin, I watched to see if she would start strong only to watch her vigor and drive wane as time went on, like I had seen in so many other people over the years. This was not the case with her. She has kept her intensity and drive consistent during her employment with the business. The story of Erin Martin is not encouraging because she is young, driven, and has a work ethic well beyond her years. Her story is encouraging because just after hire she was diagnosed with an illness that affects her entire body and often puts her into tremendous amounts of pain throughout the day and night. Often she has to get up from her desk and move around due to painful cramping and fatigue. Many times her illness keeps her up all through the night, but she still pulls herself together and brings herself to work, rarely calling in to ask for a bit of time to collect herself. Every so often, I would stop by her cubicle, check on her, and ask if she was doing well. On several occasions, she would tell me of terrible occurrences of waking up not being able to move and only being able to lie in bed and cry because of the pain. However, each time Erin worked through the pain and performed her duties at the office to the fullest of her capability because of her commitment to her core values and the Quality Paradigm in her thinking process. I have never known Erin to miss a deadline or to produce poor work. In fact, her work is widely regarded as virtually flawless. Despite any challenge, Erin does not know how to make excuses or fail. She does not know how to quit. Regarding her work, Erin Martin is a champion and positive role model to many people. She is a winner because she has the Quality Paradigm.

*Story 2:*
During my service in the United States Navy, one of my assignments was to learn how to supervise the flightline division of what was at the time the largest operational squadron in the Navy. As an aircrewman who had previously spent the better part of two years learning how to negotiate flight operations on the plane *during flight,* I was not motivated about my assignment to the Line Division to learn how to park the planes *on the ground.* I was supposed to be on the plane, not in front of it. To make things worse, the Leading Petty Officer of the Line Division was a man named AME1 Jerry Bourlet who had a reputation for being a hard-ass sailor who chewed up newbie sailors and spit them out before lunch. He was about five feet, eleven inches tall with an athletic frame, wore his salt-and-pepper hair in a well manicured flattop, and had a well-groomed mustache that did not extend past the edge of his mouth. The expression on his face at any given time gave everyone (including me) the impression he was looking for someone's ass to kick. Some people joked that he looked like a Bulldog with a bone to pick. To make matters worse, he had an especially deep dislike for "pretty-boy" aircrewman and pilots. I personally witnessed senior people (enlisted AND officers) walking towards him only to change course just to avoid having to deal with his shenanigans. A couple of times I even watched with laughter as he chased officers across the flightline just to give them some hell about not having proper hearing

protection. He was brash and loud. At times, he yelled at me constantly.

But beyond any doubt, when considering his work ethic and doing the right things right, *Jerry Bourlet was the best damn sailor I ever worked for during my entire service in the Navy*. It has taken me some years to come to this conclusion, but after close consideration, Jerry's unrelenting drive to do everything with precision and purpose is one of the largest factors that propelled me to become a successful person in my own right. Jerry had the Quality Paradigm interwoven into everything he did. His uniforms were always perfect. The shine on his boots always had a mirror-like finish. His paperwork was always correct. His attention to detail was unrelenting. His facts were always straight. His work ethic was tireless, and everyone who worked for him knew that if they worked hard and earned his respect, there was no length Jerry would not go to stand up for his sailors and reward them with an evaluation worthy of promotion.

One day I discovered that Jerry was not just a hard-assed sailor only a mother could love. I learned the tough-guy exterior came off when he left the base. AME1 Bourlet volunteered untold hours with local charities and with mentoring youth in the community. Very few people knew this about him. He never bragged about his community service. Jerry took the Quality Paradigm home with him and taught it to children in the community. He taught them excellence in everything they did and encouraged them to do everything they could do to win and to meet their potential. I am grateful that Jerry taught me to apply excellence in every area of my life, and I count myself lucky to have served with and known one of America's great Patriots. If you have half the commitment AME1 Bourlet had to doing things correctly and expecting quality outputs, your life and business would be more successful and more effective in almost every area.

I would challenge you to think about people in your own life who have taught you something through their character or their strength. So often, I find people looking for mentors and trainers to show them the keys to success when these types of teachers are all around them all of the time. Teachers and mentors are a lot like opportunity; many times, they sit openly, hiding in plain sight. Your job is to seek them out.

# WHY THIS IS THE RIGHT TIME FOR THIS BOOK

*What the people want to hear is the truth – it is the exciting thing – to speak the truth.*

- Sir Winston Churchill

Currently, our global community is in a state of crisis. Elitism and arrogance have overrun private and public sectors all over the world. Institutions the world over are refusing, at an alarming rate, to listen to constituents and customers. Businesses are quick to exchange what is right for what is immediately profitable. As a global community, we have abandoned our commitments to basic moral ideals and sound business principles so we may capture the opportunities of the moment at the expense of future stability. Unfortunately, the investment for this type of business practice is quite high and one we can never fully repay. The burden we leave to future generations of citizens and businesspeople is debt, poverty, and poorly managed institutions. Our global citizenry will polarize into the elite and the poor if we fail to progress beyond our myopic approach to everything from our interpersonal relationships to our business strategies. The middle class will vanish. The common person committed to live a decent and respectable life will become extinct. Our way of life will disappear, transfiguring into something we do not recognize. Small business will dry up; large businesses will crowd out regional interests. And the burden of governments will include too many needs and result in not enough revenue to meet their most basic responsibilities of safety and governance.

Make no mistake. I am not a doomsday prophet. I believe in the power of humanity to do the right thing and embrace the ideals and principles of genuine moral goodness that will ultimately lead to answering this world's most dire problems. This belief is one of many reasons I wrote this book. I am one concerned citizen among many in a vast global community that desires more than ever to help people become self sufficient, tap into their creative abilities, and move forward into a brighter future where families and businesses enjoy stability, the hope of prosperity, and unfettered liberty. Where there is no stability, there is no way to blossom and enjoy freedom. Instability kills our ability to dream and create innovative ways to meet challenges head-on. Each day we walk away from the Quality Paradigm, we embrace a limiting paradigm that seeks to blame others and expect the help of others concerning matters that fall squarely upon our own shoulders to negotiate. There is no silver bullet to fix all of our woes. There is no "great man" who will show up and make everything in the world perfect. That is magical thinking, and it has no basis in reality. As a global community, we can overcome our challenges when we embrace the Quality Paradigm on an individual basis and embrace our deep individual responsibility for our own behaviors and thoughts. Where there is life, liberty, and the pursuit of happiness there is integrity, honor, and responsibility. The two are inseparably conjoined and cannot survive apart from one another. We will overcome our common problems when we take individual responsibility for our lives and seek to leave the world and everyone within it better than how we found them, whenever possible.

Messages similar to mine have arisen in the past, but often with the admonition that we return backward to values we once held – as if we once lived in an imaginary golden age, when all humanity was moral and just and blind justice ruled the day. While I agree with the sentiment towards embracing a moral and just world, I disagree with the methodology of moving backwards. There was never a time in history when humanity was moral and just. Corruption has always had a part to play in our human experience. Romanticizing the past and revising history to read how we desire to see it rather than how it actually played out only serves to delude ourselves concerning the realities we face today and to cheapen the true value that principled moral pursuits offer to people's lives. The fact remains there are corrupt people in the world. There always has been. There always will be. That will never change. What can change is whether we become indifferent to our corruption and lack of personal excellence and reverse our persistent march toward selfish individualism.

This is the right time for this book because our global society has rejected the idea of moving backward to embrace the ideals of an imaginary golden age that did not exist simply because each of us knows it requires a regression, a looking back to capture an apparition that existed only in the minds of a few historical revisionists. At the risk of oversimplification, the answer to the world's challenges does not lie in moving backward. The answer lies in moving forward toward the Quality Paradigm that genuinely seeks to leave everyone and everything in a better condition than when we first found them, whenever possible.

## WHAT TO EXPECT

This book offers many different insights into many different aspects of dynamic personal leadership, personal management, organizational leadership, and organizational management as well as some of the general principles involved with the Quality Control/Quality Assurance (QC/QA) industry. This book is **not** a how-to manual concerning QC/QA methodology. For information on the specifics of creating a QC/QA program, you should seek the consultancy of someone certified and well versed in QC/QA practices for your specific industry. In doing so, make certain they use the ISO (International Organization for Standardization) regulations, standards, and best practices when constructing your quality assurance plan. I have included contact information for the American Society for Quality and the International Organization for Standardization in the resources portion of this book (for those of you outside of the United States, please consult your local quality assurance associations).

Many of the principles involved in producing quality goods and services are directly relatable to producing a quality experience in life for yourself and for your family, which is why I originally wrote this book. I simply wanted to share the pieces of wisdom and knowledge of how to excel and how to fix things that are broken through first installing a high level of quality thinking and behaving into individual leaders and managers. This book addresses both personal as well as organizational quality issues. Many practical leadership and business practices, which I derive from real situations in military and business settings, are included to illustrate how the Quality Paradigm fits into the real world each of us face each day. In writing this book, I have endeavored to tear the experience and wisdom of others and myself from the pages of real life. However, this book cannot help you if you do not apply its wisdom. None of the strategic planning, tactical planning, leadership seminars, management seminars, or academic achievement in the world will help you if you do not saturate the fabrics of your thinking processes with the Quality Paradigm. It is my sincerest hope that after you have read the book you hold in your hands you will have had as good a time in reading it as I have had in writing it. Now that we have the introduction out of the way, it is time to lay the quality foundation.

# PART I –
# A PERSONAL
# PARADIGM

# PRINCIPLE 1: A QUALITY FOUNDATION

*Integrity without knowledge is weak and useless,*
*and knowledge without integrity is dangerous and dreadful.*
- Samuel Johnson

In the beginning, there was quality, for leadership and management did not yet exist. From quality springs forth all other forms of leadership and management one could possibly imagine or develop. Without the foundation of quality, every attempt at leadership or management is nothing but hollow shells of pseudo-accomplishments leading to places of mediocrity and inefficacy.

As a global society we have become addicted to the thought of becoming better leaders or better managers, as if becoming a better leader will make us immune to all of the things that affect other people around us – you know, the mere mortals who have problems. Books and audio programs promise everything we could ever want or desire from life as the pot of gold at the end of the leadership and management rainbows. Supposedly, we can find the ultimate success (however you define it) at the end of these rainbows.

The leaders – the *"great men"* (which include women) – were supposed to lead us and manage the journey. If we would only follow the breadcrumbs dropped by the *great men,* we would all become *great men* too. If you define "great" in terms of dollars, many did become great leaders and managers. Many did find

1

the pot of gold at the end of the rainbow, but with this great treasure also travelled great consequences. Many leaders and managers have found their way to incarceration or to poverty. Many politicians have found their way to disgrace and ruin. Many sports figures have descended into disgrace by cheating on the playing field or in their personal affairs. Many average citizens have over burdened themselves by trying to emulate the lifestyles of the *great men* and inadvertently destroyed their lives in the process. For years, few said anything or issued any warning to the possibility of ruin because every follower knows you do not question the *great man*. The *great man* knows the most, has the most talent, and knows the right people. Maybe one day you can be a *great man* too. However, until then, just follow the *great man,* and everything will be fine.

I hear from people all of the time, "Where are all of the leaders? Where have they gone? Why have our *great men* fallen?" Indeed, where are all of the *great men* who were supposed to be the beacon of hope to the masses and lead us in the way we are supposed to go? There is no shortage of leadership training and focus on maximization of resources. Every Ivy League school has dynamic programs in leadership and management. Many state and private universities have excellent schools of leadership and management, as well. There should not be a vacuum of leadership in the global community, but there is a vacuum. The collapse of the global financial markets is proof of this fact. The failure of governments the world over is further proof that our capacity to control, manage, and lead the masses through challenges and crises is woefully insufficient. The social and political elite of almost every spectrum say the cause of social, political, and economical failures the world over are attributable to faulty leadership or governmental systems and that the solution to fixing each of these crises is the transition toward a different governmental model with leaders more competent to bring prosperity to the people. This perspective accomplishes one end only: to seize power and control for their interests and personal benefit while failing to address the true dynamics of our most fundamental problems. Addressing global dynamics begins by addressing personal dynamics because our problems as a global community are a reflection of our problems individually.

In many ways, humanity has grown incapable to make their own decisions. This is why we have *great men*. They make the decisions. *Great men* run the economies of the world. *Great men* lead our churches, synagogues, and mosques. The *great men* will save us. There is no more reason to think for ourselves or to develop our own intellect, character, and ethic. The *great men* will do these things for us. From the cradle to the grave, the *great men* will care for us. Our movies, books, and favorite stories are full of *great man* epics and examples that lull masses into a false sense of security. Our religions, mythologies, and superstitions are full of stories of *great men* and great saviors doing great and mighty deeds unmatched by any mere mortal. When situations become dire in each of these stories, the people call upon the *great man* (or *godly man*) to save the day. I think many believe, some on a conscious and some on a sub-conscious level, that no matter how bad things become in the world that a *great man* or a great divine savior will step in with strong leadership and power to save the day and fend off ruin. We find hope in our *great men*. Maybe this is why we find little to be hopeful about when considering ourselves? We are not *great men*. There is no place for the development of a quality character and intellect when we have a *great man* to save the day. Good enough is good enough, and the *great man* will subsidize our failures with his epic leadership and god-like qualities.

Nevertheless, what happens when the *great man* fails in his actions or fails even to show up at all? What happens when the *great man* cannot lead us to places of safety? When moments of weakness beset our *great men* and undermine their ability to lead us forward, what happens to us then? What happens to our world when situations out of anyone's control test the limits of our *great men's* ability and capacity to lead us out of harm's way? What happens when leadership fails us? What happens when the *great men* cannot provide a life of ease? What happens when we have to dig deep into ourselves and marshal the resources of work ethic, resourcefulness, courage, and character only to find that no deposits of such resources exist within us? Without a resolute commitment to the Quality Paradigm, we will continue to find disappointment. As long as "good enough is good enough," we will continue to find ruin. As long as we continue to abdicate our responsibility for executing every area of our lives with excellence, we will continue to exchange the life that is meant to be lived for one that merely existed and faded away, unnoticed. Leadership and *great men* cannot save any of us. There is a time and place for *great men* to arise and lead, and there is also a time for inspired leadership. But first we must have laid the foundation of quality into the very fabric of our society, and from there we can begin to develop effective leadership. We must strive to become nations brimming with individuals who are great and look no more for epic *great men*.

## STOP PREACHING LEADERSHIP FIRST - START PREACHING QUALITY

During my 10 weeks of Boot Camp at Naval Recruit Training Command Great Lakes, our Recruit Division Commanders (RDCs) taught us many things. However, the most important lesson they taught us was not one of leadership or management. The most important lesson they taught us was attention to detail and quality workmanship. Our RDCs gave every daily task a grade based upon how accurately we executed the evolution. Whether folding laundry or polishing boots, the RDCs wanted to know the degree of quality we produced and how accurate we had been in completing tasks. The military understands that quality must always come before leadership. Quality breeds discipline, and discipline produces higher quality. The two characters are forever linked in an unbreakable bond. Where one appears, the other is present. This book is about placing quality *before* leadership and management and applying the Quality Paradigm to your life and to your business in order to produce a better life for you, better leaders and managers for your business, and a better experience for your customers.

The concepts and principles of leadership are for leaders and people who have a potential and deep desire to become leaders. Contrary to what some leadership gurus and management trainers would like you to believe, not everyone has the emotional or intellectual fortitude to cultivate leadership and management skills. I will not concede the idea that all people have the potential for leadership. This ridiculous idea may sell seminar seats and book deals, but it is simply not true. While it *is* true that leaders are made and not born, that does not automatically qualify everyone to have equal potentiality for developing leadership and management skills. Leaders develop from the group of those men and women who have the potential and desire to learn the skills of leadership and management. Potential is a curious thing. Potential does not equal competency. Potential only means, "*You ain't done it yet.*" Many people who do have a potential to become leaders or managers never develop any competency because they never undergo any type of developmental training. We will go into further detail about this later in the book.

Quality, however, is different from leadership and management in that quality is for everyone. Quality is for the two-year old who is learning how to do things properly. Quality is for the teenager who has a list of chores and a pile of homework awaiting him or her after school. Quality is for the college student working in the lab to develop better skills. Quality is for the construction worker building us better roads. Quality is for the single mother trying to raise a family and put food on the table. Quality is for the executive trying to lead his company to the next level in the marketplace. Quality is for the athlete trying to be better than the competition. Quality has affected every single person who has ever lived before our time, affects every single person who is alive at this very moment, and will affect every single person who will ever live in the future. There is nothing more important to every area of our human existence than the idea and principles of quality. Quality is the sacred thing. Quality existed before management. Quality existed before leadership. Out of quality, sprang every good thing that has helped to perpetuate and improve our human experience. Quality is the genesis of everything that is good in this world because it forces us to produce the best ideas, workmanship, and charity that we can offer to our fellow man so we might leave them better than we found them.

## CLEARING THE BRUSH TO LAY THE FOUNDATION

Before we begin to lay the foundation of quality, we need to clear the brush and get a few facts straight. Some people like to live in strange worlds where nothing is their fault and the words "personal responsibilities" have no meaning. The first thing you need to do is to get real and stop lying to yourself. Take off the blinders or the rose-colored glasses and look at the world around you and the world you have created for yourself. Put down the excuse-encrusted filter through which you see the world as a cruel taskmaster and look in the mirror at the true problem: **You.**

The problem is not your boss, whether he is an asshole or not; the problem is how you choose to react to him. The problem is not that your spouse is cruel and inattentive; you married him or her, and regardless of why, you choose to stay in the marriage that does not work. The problem you have with disciplining your children does not begin with your children; had you been a better and more involved parent when they were younger, many of the problems you face now might not be problems. The problem is not the business partner who robbed you blind; the problem is the fact you failed to set checks and balances in place to insure this sort of thing would not happen (I know this first hand from my own failure in this area). Additionally, you probably trusted someone who you knew or should have known could not be trusted. An old-fashioned dose of Reagan wisdom could have saved you a lot of pain and money: *trust, but verify.* The fact you overdrew your accounts is not the bank's fault; you should have kept a closer eye on your financial situation. When the cop pulled you over for speeding, he wasn't being an asshole – you were the one speeding. Why is he the asshole for catching you breaking the law? Are you kidding me?

Stop playing the victim. Stop making excuses for everything wrong in your life and taking credit for everything that is right. You have the exercise backwards. You are supposed to share your wins and own your shortcomings. Stop trying to give everything meaning or a story explaining why it is the way it is so you can feel secure and explain it away. Not everything has a reason or even needs a reason. Some things are just the way they are for reasons that cannot be determined or do not really matter in the big scope of life. Sometimes shit just happens. Get over it. Take control of your world by taking responsibility for every aspect that comprises your life. It is not everyone else's fault for where you are along life's journey. The fault lies with how you chose to react to those things that happened to you in your past and how you choose to address situations that challenge you today.

Before we discuss quality, leadership, management, relationships, finances, or anything else that pertains to your life, we need to clear the brush and establish a couple of ground rules. These ground rules are simple. They provide a smooth place on which to lay a foundation for establishing the Quality Paradigm in your life.

1. **No excuses**: Do not accept excuses from yourself or anyone else. An excuse-maker is someone who fabricates a false world that does not exist in an effort to justify escaping from his or her responsibility or reality. In the real world, the establishment of who is at fault for events that happen to you is a fool's errand and does nothing to address the situation at hand. The first and best question to ask is, "What is my responsibility in regard to this event?" Once you know what your responsibility is in the matter, you are now in a position to hold other people involved responsible for their part in the event. The event may not be your fault, but it is your responsibility to manage your response. A lack of fault does not abdicate you from your responsibilities to yourself or to others. It does not matter whose fault something is because you are ultimately responsible for you.

2. **No extremes**: Do not be sucked into the dark hole of negativity and pessimism or the blinding light of dopy optimism. By dopy optimism, I mean an unrealistic belief that no matter the event everything is going to be all right. That's bullshit, and you know it. People who believe this are trying to ignore problems with the hope that either they will go away or someone else will rescue them (perhaps a *great man*?). If you do not take care of business and see the world around you as it is, life is going to hammer you. Just because you believe it is going to be all right in the end does not make it true (we will discuss this later in Chapter 2). If you choose to hang on to this dopy optimism, the best

advice I can give to you is to duck and cover because you probably have major problems headed your way. The balance is to be an optimistic realist. The glass is *not* half-empty, and the glass is *not* half-full. The glass is simply filled halfway, and if we can get some more water, we can have a glass that is filled to its capacity. The optimistic realist will look at any situation and say, "It is what it is, but I believe there are opportunities we can capture here if we take the time to look for them. How can we make this situation work for us in the long term while addressing the current liabilities and preventing future liabilities in the short term?" It has been said repeatedly by gurus the world over – you have to face it to replace it. If you keep it between the lines and resist the urge to get into extremes, you will be able to do both – face it and replace it.

3. **No Drama**: No drama means just what it says – no drama. You will not win any awards for dramatic acting in the real world. Not everything that happens in your life is a crisis. Think about it, if everything were a crisis, *nothing would be a crisis.* I apply this rule to my life in everything I set out to do and everything that happens to me. Very few things are crises in my life for the simple reason that very few events are truly life or death. Are financial catastrophes a crisis? Maybe they are, maybe they are not. It depends on the context and long-term consequences. What about an automobile accident? Is that a crisis? It all depends on the entirety of the situation and condition surrounding the crash. In stressful situations, if you freak out and create unnecessary drama out of the problem, the situation will only become worse and more confusing. You will lose sight of what is really going on. This is why it is best to keep calm with a cool head at all times and keep things in their proper context. The no-drama rule also prevents you from creating drama unnecessarily. I used to know a man, whom we will call John, who was addicted to creating drama. John was not content

with peacefulness and never felt secure unless there was a fire afoot. Many times I witnessed this man create problems with colleagues and friends just so he would have something to gossip and fume about. At other times, he would intentionally create (either consciously or unconsciously I do not know) problems to which only he could be the answer. The only purpose this served to accomplish was the confirmation in his own mind that he was an amazing leader and problem solver (in addition to his flair for the dramatic, he was an unabashed narcissist). All the while, his peers and superiors viewed him as an idiot, and few people took him seriously for any length of time. How do you know a crisis from a non-crisis? You will know a crisis by the severity and breadth of the consequences. Whether a crisis or not, do not allow drama to creep in, ever. It is best to leave the drama to the professionals on the stage and the silver screen.

These are the three basic ground rules you must embrace before you begin to build the Quality Paradigm in your own life. Do not allow yourself to be a party to excuses, extremes, or drama for any reason – ever – because they will conspire against you and assassinate any attempt to be successful long term.

## THE MATTER OF QUALITY

Everything in the universe is comprised of matter. Generally, the definition of matter is anything that has a mass and a volume. However, inanimate ideas have matter as well, although admittedly not in the scientific sense of the word. You cannot measure an idea with a scale or calculate the physical volume an idea consumes. However, ideas have something very similar to matter. They have essence. The essence of an idea is what makes the idea what it is and gives it fullness and life in both the minds of the communicator and the hearer. Ideas have the potential to change the world, your business, and your life. The idea of quality is no different. The essence of quality is split into different parts, all of which come together to comprise the whole idea. The virtues that make up the essence of quality can help us to understand what quality truly means to ourselves, our clients, businesses, products, friends and family, our countries, and our own communities.

## HONOR

*Who sows virtue reaps honor.*

- Leonardo da Vinci

I am convinced that comparatively few people remain in the world who have a deep sense or conscious attention to developing and maintaining honor. Many people develop different aspects of honor such as integrity, courage, loyalty, or a sense of selfless service, but few people seek diligently to develop the fullness of character that constitutes being truly honorable. We refer to elected officials and judges as honorable because of their positions, but this is not what makes a man or women honorable. The title of honorable (or the like) signifies high respect, and yet as a global community, we have allowed the honorable among us to display less than honorable behavior and still maintain their titles. As a parent, I deeply understand my responsibility to be the type of man and father my daughters will want to honor and to respect. What follows then is their natural respect for my influence in their lives. I strive to walk honorably before my children (and admittedly have often fallen short) and only require the honor or respect from them that I have earned. To be respected, you must be respectable. To be honored, you must first demonstrate you are honorable. Being an honorable person comes at the high cost of personal discipline and commitment to say no to selfish and destructive behaviors and habits that others find acceptable in regards to their personal and professional conduct.

Becoming an honorable person means making a decision to demonstrate in your conduct a commitment to self respect and respect of your fellow man; a sense of devotion to your family, your friends, your business, and your co-workers; and an affinity for personal courage when making the hard decisions or confronting wrong doers and those oppressing the weak among us. An honorable person conducts himself or herself to the very utmost of their ability in an ethical manner in each of their many relationships; seeks to take personal responsibility for failures and mistakes no matter how grave or seemingly insignificant; and never allows others to be blamed when the responsibility does not reasonably fall to them. Possessing a deep sense of honor means always seeking for ways to leave the world around you in a better condition, whenever possible, than how you found it.

## COURAGE

*We must build dikes of courage to hold back the flood of fear.*

### - Dr. Martin Luther King, Jr.

When you find courage, it will be in two forms and have countless applications. The two forms of courage found in the world are physical courage and moral (intellectual) courage. Physical courage requires those acts where heroes run into burning buildings or citizens stop an act of violence in order to save lives. These acts often put oneself into physical danger or serve to protect others with little or no regard for personal safety. We see examples of courage everyday in newspapers and television reports about hometown and military heroes serving others and often paying the ultimate cost so that others might live. These physical acts of courage are often shadows cast by the substance of an inner moral courage that drives the behavior and decision-making processes of the hero.

Physical courage generally and moral courage specifically are parts of the concrete mixture that serves as the foundation of the Quality Paradigm. Moral courage is the ability of a person to act upon those principles of honor, commitment, loyalty, duty, respect, sacrifice, integrity, and excellence regardless of the personal, emotional, or professional pressures of their environment. It means adhering to and giving voice to closely held values in either benign or hostile situations. People must learn to hold the values that make up the essence of quality in higher esteem than any other ideal and keep them in the place of highest honor in their life and in their society. When we fail to hold in high regard the values of the essence of quality, we fail to exhibit the moral courage required to live a life dedicated to leaving everything and everyone better than we found them. Moral courage ignores profit and loss and personal consequence, and it defers to the higher calling of our values. Where a person finds their value system is not as important as whether the value system they embrace serves to make them a better person and their world a better place than how they found it.

## COMMITMENT

*There are only two options regarding commitment. You're either in or out. There's no such thing as a life in-between.*

- Pat Riley

The value of commitment is the ingredient that drives a person to be "all in." The Quality Paradigm leaves no room to be lukewarm or uncommitted regarding our immediate responsibilities. Nowhere is this more important than family. A deep commitment to assuring the protection and prosperity of your family is paramount and central to the overall idea of being a person of value. Commitment means keeping first things first and striving each day to keep the many facets of your life in delicate balance.

Speaking from personal experience, I have endeavored since my first child was born to be a father that never sacrificed my relationship with my children for advancement or reward from my business. I saw very early that time and money, though important aspects of relationships are not the currency of relationships. The currency of relationships, especially familial relationships, is communicating a deep sense of commitment to others through honesty, authenticity, and making meaningful intellectual, spiritual, and emotional deposits. Over the past 13 years, there have been times I have been gone from my family for six or more months at a time, yet I never missed an opportunity to communicate my commitment to my children through cards, letters, conversations, and stories that illustrated meaningful ideals. The distance between us could never diminish or otherwise render worthless the currency of commitment in my relationship with my children. Today, my daughters and I share a deep bond of love, mutual respect, and deep admiration. Daily deposits of commitment funded the purchase of this special relationship.

Beyond your commitment to your family, you should have a deep sense of commitment to your employer, your business, and your employees, and to each of your clients. In the age of job-hopping and trying to find the next best thing in the job market, as a society, we have largely abandoned our commitments to our employers and businesses. Employees have become cynical of the idea of committing long-term to an employer because the marketplace has taught workers to be skeptical of businesses' loyalty to their employees, and for good reason. All too often, businesses have sacrificed their employees and business partners on the altar of greed in the name of preserving shareholder profits and doing what was best for the business. Making a decision that may be right by the numbers must never trump the right decision concerning your human capital. I am not naïve to the realities of business and times that call for making the tough decisions regarding employment levels. I am referring to those times companies knowingly break their commitments to employees who serve their employers well and deserve fair treatment but instead are treated as an expendable commodity and tossed aside. There must be a mutual commitment between you and your employer or business. Both must commit to providing the other with specific benefits. Employment and business relationships are like any other relationship – they must be mutually beneficial to be ultimately profitable, or else they will stagnate and become co-dependent or worse. As I write this book, the world is engaged in a financial struggle unlike any seen for generations. The stench of fear permeates the marketplace and serves to remind employees and employers alike that no businesses and no jobs are safe. It is in these times we must pull together, renew our mutual commitments, and perform them with honor.

Beyond our commitments to our family and our employer or business, we must be committed to leaving our fellow citizens within our local, national, and international communities in a better condition, whenever possible, than how we first found them. Feeding the hungry across the globe is fine, but have you gazed so far across the globe that you have blurred your vision to those who are hungry across the street? Have you showed more commitment to those hurting elsewhere that you have overlooked those hurting in your own community? The Quality Paradigm drives people to be involved in their communities, their countries, and their world – in that order. Those in your community can affect you most immediately. I will never forget the affect feeding and serving the homeless in the Seattle metro area had on my two young daughters. Week after week they served the people who were less fortunate but no less human. This experience taught them to appreciate what they have and never forget to reach out to those in need. In fact, my youngest daughter still talks about the times she handed out milk to people and how nice they were. She was able to see the humanity through the misery and to brighten an otherwise darkened life. Committing to make a difference in some way to your local community serves as a stepping-stone to joining the conversation concerning the national narrative. Involvement with national organizations then provides opportunities to address global issues. But ultimately, your commitment to your fellow citizens should begin in your local community.

## LOYALTY

*Every society rests in the last resort on the recognition of common principles and common ideals, and if it makes no moral or spiritual appeal to the loyalty of its members, it must inevitably fall to pieces.*

- Christopher Dawson

Loyalty, for our purposes, is akin to commitment but not quite the same. One can be committed to a person, a group of people, or a cause but not be exclusively loyal to it. A person may be loyal physically and demonstrate commitment to a relationship or cause but disloyal in their thoughts and private intentions. Additionally, one may be committed to a cause but not be exclusively loyal to furthering only that particular cause. In business, an employee may be wholly committed to coming to work each day and doing his or her very best because of their deep sense of work ethic and self-discipline while having absolutely no loyalty to the company whatsoever. The first opportunity to leave for a better position or more money will draw this committed employee to be loyal to his or her own interests at the expense of the company's interests. In the example above concerning the employee, the employee is not being disloyal since he probably never made an initial agreement to be loyal to the company at the expense of his own well-being in the first place.

Many, if not most, relationships need only to be committed

in equal portion. An over-commitment from one side or the other brings a situation where someone is over-committed and that someone is going to get hurt. **Never make a commitment to someone who or something that considers you an option.** Ever. Additionally, never become loyal to a person or a cause to a degree that is unequal to the degree of loyalty they return in kind. Loyalty requires a mutual accountability, and you should extend it very carefully and only after an ample amount of time has been spent developing deep levels of trust and the demonstration of loyal and committed behavior.

What makes loyalty different from commitment is that loyalty requires a deep and meaningful emotional attachment followed by behavior that demonstrates that loyalty, whereas commitment lacks the necessity of an emotional attachment, and you may judge it solely upon demonstrable behavior. If I am loyal to you, my behavior will be toward your benefit despite personal expense to me. The degree of loyalty determines the degree of personal expense I am willing to endure up to and including my life (which is a level of loyalty you should reserve only for those people and ideals most dear to you). If I am committed to you but loyal to another, my behavior will be toward your benefit until such time that it conflicts with my personal loyalties that lie elsewhere. To avoid conflicts between your commitments and your loyalties, choose your personal loyalties very carefully and keep them few in number. Loyalty is a deep virtue best balanced thoughtfully.

## DUTY

*Rights that do not flow from duty well performed are not worth having.*

- Mohandas Gandhi

The Quality Paradigm requires a strong sense of duty, which is to say a deep commitment to fulfill your obligations to the very utmost of your abilities as required by the task. The value of duty is the driving internal obligation of a person to fulfill his or her commitments properly. Duty is the mechanism whereby loyalty and commitment translate into their behavioral equivalents. Duty is an action word. The man or woman of words without purposed action is the person who lacks true loyalty and commitment to another or to a stated cause. Duty encompasses the idea of work ethic, and the Quality Paradigm leaves no room to take short cuts or to skip steps in the process of getting things done correctly. Nowhere was this more apparent to me than on the flightline during my years in the Navy. The sailors and aircrewman who perform maintenance on the Navy's aircraft have a deep sense of duty to each other and to their Command, which compels them to perform each maintenance effort according to the steps prescribed by their technical manuals. These men and women hold each other accountable to make sure each member of the team performs his or her duties to this high standard because people's lives depend on it.

Regardless of whether you enjoy your work, you have an obligation – a duty to perform your assigned tasks to the utmost of your ability. If you feel you cannot fulfill that obligation day in and day out where you currently work, you must find a job where you can perform your tasks to this level. The Quality Paradigm leaves no allowance for the performance of tasks to be "good enough." The application of the Quality Paradigm and the sense of duty that accompanies these ideals demands devotion of the best effort on every task every time. A sense of duty applies to everything we do for our families and for our employers or companies. You have a duty to your children to raise them in such a way as to benefit them and prepare them for adulthood and to be a productive and responsible part of society. You have a duty to your spouse or partner to provide value to the household and to share in the successes and failures and challenges and triumphs of your family unit and your relationships. You have a duty to yourself to give the best part of your talents to everything you do and to sign your life's work with the signature of excellence.

## RESPECT

*Knowledge will give you power, but character, respect.*

- Bruce Lee

We live in a world where pop-culture tells us that in order for others to take notice of our talent we must continue to raise the bar (or lower the bar depending upon how you view it) of public antics or our often lewd personal conduct. Our computers, televisions, and radios feed us a constant stream of people who publically humiliate themselves in displays of shameless idiocy in order to capture their 15 minutes of fame. As a culture, Americans have largely lost their sense of class and self-respect. Can you blame them? It has been at least one generation since anyone has thought to teach children the idea of building and maintaining a good family name or a good personal reputation. In my opinion, the basic lack of self-respect and regard for building a respectable family name is due in large part to the degradation of the family unit in the past 20 to 30 years. Due to the degradation of the family unit, our children simply do not have a family name of which to be proud. When parents fail to act with honor and courage and perform their solemn duty to fulfill their roles as parents, guardians, role models, and wise counsels, someone or something (such as drugs, alcohol, unprotected sex, destructive behavior, or other destructive influence) becomes a guiding factor in how children view themselves and the world in which they live.

Our current generation largely believes that the amount of money one has in one's possession determines the amount of respect one should be given. While it is true that affluence does command a certain level of respect, it can never replace the deeply rooted respect an honorable character commands. Affluence demands a respect of power that money affords, while a strong character demands a personal respect that wins the hearts and minds of family, friends, and colleagues regardless of the balance of your financial accounts. Affluence only commands respect so long as the money is present. If you take away the money, the respect disappears, and thus this type of respect is a false respect - a respect that appears real but is not. When you come to a place in your life where you have affluence and a strong personal character, this is a most potent combination that will afford you many opportunities to leave a positive impact on the world around you by leaving it in a better condition than how you first found it.

The first respect one must possess is self-respect because the law of respect says you teach other people how to treat you through your personal conduct. When you respect you, I will respect you.

If I fail to respect you when you have done nothing to warrant a lack of respect, you are likely to disassociate yourself with me (as well you should). Self-respect is not arrogance. Arrogance is a regard for oneself that is neither earned nor warranted. It is a gross over estimation of one's value and often serves as a cover for the empty and insecure child that screams inside. Arrogant people are not strong people. They are generally weak morally, easy to manipulate and overcome through appealing to their egos and appetite for attention. Self-respect is like any other type of respect. It is the social currency of life, and just like its monetary cousin – **you must earn it**. Earning respect for yourself begins by simply keeping your word to yourself and striving to see the world as it truly is. Being honest about yourself and the conditions in which one finds himself or herself is the bedrock of self-respect. Keeping your word to yourself will teach you to trust your instincts and ability to make sound decisions. It brings with it an authentic confidence that is required for long-term success.

What follows self-respect is the respect of others. I can never truly respect you unless I truly respect myself. Respecting others and regarding others according to their station in life is important for determining personal conduct. If you were in a room full of men and women of great accomplishment and public esteem, it would be disrespectful to approach any of them and try to give them a high-five and speak to them in a familiar manner, especially if you had never met their acquaintance. Your blatant disregard for their accomplishments and personal character would be most insulting. It would indicate that you know neither self-respect nor respect of others and that you serve as the center of your selfish world. Respecting others means respecting their accomplishments, their possessions, their character, their reputation, their opinions (even if you happen to disagree with their positions), and their interests. Respecting others demands that when we disagree, we do not become disagreeable and rude. Treating others with respect regardless of their station in life reflects more upon your character than it does the character of the other. All people deserve your respect initially until such time that they teach you through their disrespectful conduct that your respect is no longer warranted. The Quality Paradigm demands that we treat all people with a basic level of respect and that we disassociate ourselves from people whom we have observed to be disrespectful of themselves and of others.

## SACRIFICE (SERVICE)

*If we do not lay out ourselves in the service of mankind whom should we serve?*

- John Adams

The virtue of sacrifice is what compels people all over the world to put the good of the many before the good of the few or the one. The men and women who serve honorably in the military understand sacrifice better than anyone else I have come across. Not only do the service members understand sacrifice, their families understand what it means to sacrifice personal well-being for the good of the many. This is why we take great pains to honor service members and their families in this nation.

Not everyone is eligible to serve in the military, but that does not mean you do not have the opportunity to serve others. Instead of sitting at home weekend after weekend spending time watching the television, gather your children together and find an organization that is committed to meeting a need in your community that really draws at your heart. For several years, our family fed the homeless and counseled with people who had suffered abuse, addiction, and/or alcoholism. This was our way of sacrificing time and resources for the good of the community. What present needs exist in your local community that your family can sacrifice a small amount of time and resources to address? Group sacrifice often creates lasting bonds of friendship, trust, and love between people and between communities. In fact, of all of the ingredients to meeting the needs of a hurting world, sacrifice is the indispensible ingredient. Without *shared* proportional sacrifice across social, economic, political, religious, and racial lines, there can be no lasting answer to the world's most pressing challenges.

Sacrifice comes in other forms as well, especially in relation to areas of personal and professional responsibility. Those who go the extra mile are a prime example of people who exhibit personal sacrifice in order to meet the needs of his or her employer and their clients. Often I have seen these types of people come to the office on their days off because of their commitment to make sure they take care of their areas of responsibility. These sacrifices have a direct impact on the profitability of their company. Sacrifice goes beyond scheduled hours and drives us to address issues based upon the priority of the need rather than our immediate desires. By sacrifice, I do not mean to convey the unhealthy co-dependence, also known as "the victim," role that many people play and try to masquerade as sacrifice. Never one time have I observed a person who exhibits genuine sacrifice play the victim role in the office or in their personal affairs. Daily, they demonstrate personal leadership and then attend diligently to their professional responsibilities. With responsibility comes sacrifice, but with sacrifice comes eventual reward. Patience and sacrifice are siblings who travel together. Where one is present, the other is always close at hand.

## INTEGRITY

*Calamity is the test of integrity.*

- Samuel Richardson

The idea of integrity as it relates to ethics and personal conduct means to convey wholeness and cohesion, not perfection. Personal integrity is a matter of character and serves to be the road upon which consistent top-performance travels. I have known many men and women whom I would consider to demonstrate consistent personal and professional integrity. None of these individuals is perfect, and each of them suffered their own personal and professional challenges due to poor decisions at one time or another. However, though they have suffered challenges, they have managed to avoid making the *big* mistakes by choosing instead to use wisdom and moderation in their conduct. People of integrity admit shortcomings and work diligently to address them without sacrificing their good-standing reputation.

Often our society creates demigods out of our heroes and stars (resulting from of our need for a *great man*) while chasing after them daily, watching, often hoping, to catch them in a moment of impropriety or weakness. We cast down these demigods when we catch them and brand them with an unseen scarlet letter, stripping them of their dignity. Often, this results from the fiendish idea that people who demonstrate integrity must adhere *perfectly* to some set of moral absolutes as dictated by unwritten social mores or more commonly antiquated religious dictums. This behavior is unfair and often destructive, but it accomplishes the goal of placing oneself as judge, jury, and executioner of others in society. It is a ridiculous exercise, yet an exercise from which humanity cannot seem to get away.

Humanity engages in this sort of unhealthy self-justification because each of us has to look into the mirror everyday at the person we know has acted with impropriety and weakness of character. Almost all people want others to view them as being a person of character and integrity. When we fail in our own eyes or somehow come to believe for whatever reason that we do not measure up to the expectation of our social or religious rules and traditions we create an inequality between others and ourselves. We create a moral deficit that we perceive to be insurmountable. To address the perceived inequality often it is easier (certainly more convenient) to justify our actions by bringing others down to the level we believe we now must live due to our personal shortcomings. People who demonstrate integrity suffer these same temptations to create a moral deficit but instead decide against responding negatively and take action to correct their poor decisions and thus repair and re-elevate their ethical standard.

People of integrity are like everyone else with a few exceptions:
1. They strive to hold themselves to a high ethical standard.
2. They immediately take responsibility for their actions when they fall short.
3. They move quickly to address the consequences of the behaviors or poor decisions.

People who lack integrity engage in a few different types of self-delusion:
1. They try to draw others around them down to a level on which they perceive themselves to exist presently.
2. They justify or deny their actions.
3. They simply find fault with everyone around them in an exercise of self-justification and marginalization.

The Quality Paradigm dictates that all personal and professional conduct is in keeping with the highest values of our respective societal norms and professions, and when (not if) we fail to keep those high standards, we immediately take responsibility for our conduct and move to make reparations as required. Consistency of ethical conduct is the essence of integrity and an absolutely essential piece to developing the Quality Paradigm in your life.

## EXCELLENCE

*Be a yardstick of quality. Some people aren't used to an environment where excellence is expected.*

- Steve Jobs

Excellence derives largely from a passion and commitment to seek better ways to address the always-present challenges each of us face day to day in every area of our lives personally and professionally. While we may strive to be excellent and to demonstrate excellence in our conduct and attitudes, it is important that we do not become overly zealous in our pursuit of excellence and stray into the deep weeds of arrogance and elitism. Elitism, when used pejoratively, creates an illusion that one person or group of people is inherently more deserving or intellectually more able than other people or groups. It loses sight of personal interrogation and growth, often leaning on pedigree or previous accomplishment. Excellence does no such thing. Excellence understands each day as unique, and each day's efforts must be sufficient to meet present challenges. The feeling of being elite or superior is a cruel condition that blinds the eyes of otherwise capable people to the possibility, consequence, or probability of challenges. It also has the tendency to exchange creativity and resourcefulness for establishment thinking and entitlement.

There can be no quality without excellence. There is no way to meet your own expectations or the expectations of clients and customers without tightly embracing excellence and weaving it into the fabric of each endeavor. The Quality Paradigm dictates that good enough is never good enough for people who embrace and employ excellence in every area of their lives. Individual commitments to excellence within any organization will soon create a positively charged and innovative culture of excellence that is contagious. While serving in the Navy, I was assigned to Fleet Air Reconnaissance Squadron One (VQ-1) and was introduced to a culture of excellence in a degree I had yet to previously encounter. The men and women who maintain the aircrafts at VQ-1 are known simply as *"the professionals"* because professionals are committed to excellence and executing the correct tasks correctly. Each day at VQ-1, our aircrews and maintenance crews worked diligently to meet each demand and to address these demands with excellence. There was only one way to do anything at VQ-1: *the right way.* By embracing the Quality Paradigm, you are dedicating yourself always to do everything you endeavor the same way – with excellence.

## CONCLUDING THOUGHTS

The Quality Paradigm is the genesis of effective leadership and management that will also serve as the lodestar of future generations. Collective greatness begins with personal greatness. When countries are great it is because their people were great beforehand. When we crown a champion on the field, it is because he or she was first a champion in the gym. Both of my daughters have worked very hard at learning and achieving high scholastic marks. I remember the semester before my oldest daughter brought home straight A's for the first time; I would tell her to earn the grades she desired to have at the end of the semester everyday during the semester. If she was to attain her goal, her daily behavior had to align with the outcome she desired. Both of my daughters have embraced that idea and subsequently earned their spots on the Honor Role and the National Honor Society. Success begins in your mind. It begins with how you think about everything around you and how you view your role in relation to where you would like to end up at the end of this season of your life. Striving to leave everything and everyone you meet in a better condition than how you first encountered them will enable you achieve the larger goal of creating the life you would like to live, instead of settling for the life you were told you should live.

Now that we have laid a quality foundation, it is time to learn the truth about the enemy of the limiting paradigm.

# PRINCIPLE 2: DESTROYING THE LIMITING PARADIGM

*So let me assert my firm belief that the only thing we have to fear is fear itself – nameless, unreasoning, unjustified terror that paralyzes needed efforts to convert retreat into advance.*

- Franklin D. Roosevelt

## THE LIMITING PARADIGM

As you know by now, the essence of the Quality Paradigm in your life is leaving everyone and everything in a better condition than how you first encountered them. The limiting paradigm is an insidious enemy to the Quality Paradigm and a toxic hazard to the overall idea of a quality mindset. These two distinctly different thinking processes are mutually exclusive and diametrically opposed in every way possible. The limiting paradigm is quite simply negativity and fear that invade open minds without gates of self-discipline to keep the mind safe from attack, resulting in behaviors and opinions that ultimately sabotage other people's attempts to produce a quality lifestyle for them and for others. The limiting paradigm leaves a stain on the minds of men and women all over the world. Men and women who are leaders in the business marketplace understand how important it is to keep a clear head focused on possibilities and solutions while shutting out negativity and toxic people. Toxic people are everywhere. In fact, the mentalities of most people are toxic to the potentially successful, which explains why so few people actually achieve their goals.

The biggest differences between the achievers and the average person has nothing to do with money, influence, power, upbringing, luck, or anything else that is credited for people's successes. The biggest difference between the two groups is that the thinking processes of the average person concerning themselves and their dreams are usually negative, and the average person has distinctly different behavioral patterns than the achiever's group. The thinking and the acting do not align with the dreaming. Their thinking creates barriers that they do not believe they can overcome. This breeds a host of negative emotions like jealousy, frustration, anger, depression, indifference, worry, doubt, criticism, and just about any other negative emotion you could name. It is a lot like chasing sunsets while facing east. If I am chasing sunsets while running east, it does not matter how badly I want to see a sunset because my faulty thinking (assuming the sun sets in the east when it really sets in the west) and my faulty actions (running east instead of west) will never align with what I say I desire.

When I used to coach and counsel the addicted, the abused, and the homeless in the Seattle, Washington area, often they would speak of all of the dreams they wanted to accomplish instead of being drunk, high, or living in an abusive situation. While I am very aware that there are physiological urges that drive people involved with these sorts of behavior to continue in their addictions or otherwise destructive situations, much of their problem lay within their mind and their inability to believe that they can be free from the addiction. Between an automatic or predisposed physical yearning and a negative outlook, most of these people have little to no chance of success. All of the men and women who were successful at beating their addictions had a paradigm shift at a pivotal point concerning their capacity to overcome these addictions, and they learned new behaviors to facilitate the recovery. These people displayed the ability to do a 180-degree turn, head west into the sunset, and many times experience a happily ever after ending.

My use of addiction as an example is intentional. Toxic, negative people are addicted to their limiting paradigm and their poor behavioral choices. People behave in such a way that works for them and helps them to have what they believe they deserve. Notice I said, "believe they deserve" instead of "say they deserve." This subtle difference is quite apparent in toxic people. Toxic people usually say they deserve to have the finer things in life. They say they want to have riches, the corner office, and a successful career, but their actions tell a much different story about what they truly believe concerning themselves. People who truly believe they deserve the better things in life take purposed action to make sure their behaviors align with their core beliefs. For instance, if you have a negative view of money because you were taught your entire childhood that the love of money was the root of all evil, it is highly probable that you will have feelings of guilt when you begin to act in a way that causes you to earn lots of money. Subconsciously, (if you have any ethical standard whatsoever) your mind does not want to be evil, and if focusing on and having money means you have done something morally wrong, it will cause internal conflict, frustration, guilt, and ultimately limited thinking and behaviors. This sort of intellectual and emotional toxicity is highly contagious and almost impossible to hide once it takes hold of your mind. Be very careful of the opinions you allow your mind to entertain.

The limiting paradigm sees all of the boulders that block the way to the summit. The limiting paradigm sees all of the reasons the accomplishment of a goal is not possible. The limiting paradigm sees all the reasons you cannot succeed and achieve your dreams. Why is opening that business impossible? Why do you not deserve a handsome husband or a beautiful wife? What reason could you possibly have for settling for an abusive or neglecting significant other? Why do you go into your office day after day and work for people who could not care whether you lived or died? For the money? Are you kidding me? If your dreams have such little worth that you would willingly stay in a situation like that rather than pursue your dreams, your dreams probably are not worth pursuing anyway. Dream bigger. Be bolder. No one who genuinely seeks to better themselves and others around them deserves the reality of a never ending day-in and day-out existence. I am talking about the average person who gets up every day, looks into the mirror, and wonders why his life is not what he dreamed it would be when he was a child. I am talking about the faithful worker who trudges into the office, performs their work with excellence, and receives no recognition year after year. Are you living the life you deserve, or are you settling for the life of one who carries the limiting paradigm? There is more to life, and you can find it beyond the threshold of the Quality Paradigm.

What about the achievers who have houses, cars, and boats and live what the average person would consider the American Dream? Are their lives free of problems? Do they feel fulfillment in everything they do? Hardly. Everyone has problems, and everyone has areas of their lives that they find unfulfilling. In fact, many of the people who live the American Dream are just as unhappy and just as discouraged and infected with toxic thinking as anyone else. The only difference is their earning ability. The limiting paradigm does not care about your social status or bank balance. This emptiness comes from people not feeling like they are contributing to anything that has meaning. The Quality Paradigm is about having meaning and purpose in life. I hear people many times say they are looking for the meaning of life. That is a fool's errand. Life has no inherent meaning. Life just *is*. When it is gone, it is gone. There is no way to call for a mulligan in life. You get one shot, and that is it. You give your life whatever meaning you decide it should have. Your behaviors are the paintbrushes you use to color every area of your life and give meaning and fulfillment to your experiences. *You* give your life color and depth. *You* paint bright colors in the lives of people around you and in your own life. *You* **give the meaning to life that you believe you deserve to have.** Killing the limiting paradigm begins by reevaluating what you believe about yourself. It begins with changing the optics of your mind's eye through developing self-respect and the nine traits that comprise the essence of a quality paradigm we outlined in Chapter 1. I say developing self-respect instead of developing self-esteem because self-esteem is simply how one thinks about oneself regardless of whether the view has any merit. Esteem is something anyone can have, which makes it valueless because nothing is given in exchange for it. Not so with respect. You *earn* respect. You pay for it through developing character and respectable conduct and behaviors. Likewise, you earn self-respect. You can have no more and no less of it than what your behavior demands. You earn your own respect as well as that of others.

# THE LIMITING PARADIGM IN BUSINESSES

Business cultures are an extension and a net amalgamation of the most influential personalities that make up the whole of the organization. This amalgamation creates a culture that is unique to that particular company, and no other corporate culture is quite the same. In many ways, companies are identical to individuals and exhibit the same behaviors. Often, the environment of a business's market will shape the culture, behaviors, and practices of the organization because the business wants to meet the demands of its clients. It wants to create acceptance, just as individuals want to be accepted. With individuals, their environment influences behaviors that in turn create a culture within a larger group of individuals because people generally desire to fit in and find acceptance. Even with the influence of environment, companies have a choice of how they respond to difficult conditions or unique challenges. Businesses face market pressure in the same way individuals face peer pressure. In the moment between an event and its effect, companies choose how they will allow the event to affect their organization. Businesses choose responses in the same way individuals choose responses. This moment in time between the event and the response can become a pivotal point that defines the organization for years to come.

The fish rots from the head down, and so do organizations. This is not a new or original idea, but it is no less true today than when first spoken centuries ago. While the generally accepted interpretation of this statement is a reference to corruption or incompetence, it can also refer to the limiting paradigm that destroys a company's ability to conduct effectively the research and development of new and innovative ideas. Toxic thinking in the leadership and senior management of any organization will eventually pollute the entire business. If you own a small- or medium-sized business, allowing negative thinking and toxic personalities into high levels of management will likely result in degraded output and possibly fatal mistakes. Toxicity destroys everything within a business. Toxicity destroys inspired thinking. Toxicity brings with it dark clouds that blot out the sunshine of creative possibility.

# THINKING PROCESSES

Clearing your mind's eye and taking control of your thinking processes are to take control of your whole being. Everything from the gate of your step to the expressions on your face and the inflection of your voice is a result of the internal state of your mind. Few things are more central to your chances of success than your mental state. In fact, I cannot think of one thing more important to your success than your overall mindset. The Quality Paradigm seeks to leave everyone and everything in a better position than how you first became involved with them. To do this, you have to have a positive and realistic frame of mind. You must make a great effort to capture negative or counterproductive thinking before they lead to destructive or counterproductive behaviors. You will ultimately act upon those thoughts that you think about most often and believe. Some people do not see how the preceding sentence can be true when all they seem to think about is writing that book, making that record, opening that business, or some other goal that keeps them up at night. The problem is not in their dreaming. The problem is in all of the other things they are thinking about in the background while they are dreaming. You know, the "buts":

> I am going to write that book one day, *but* I just do not have the time right now.

> I am going to record that album, *but* I do not have the money to do it right now. I will just wait.

> I am going to leave this damn cubicle and finally open my own business, *but* the market is very bad right now, and I am not even sure if anyone would want to buy my product or service anyway. *Besides* my spouse would freak out and make my life hell.

> I am going to go back to college and finish that degree, *but* I am probably too old to do it now. *Besides*, I was never very good at school anyway.

> I would love to start an interior design business, *but* I am just not sure I could do it.

I would love to get out of this dead-end relationship, *but* then I would be alone, and I am not sure I could handle life by myself.

I would love to be a people person, *but* people just do not seem to like me, and I do not want to change.

I would love to be successful like other people in my family, *but* I am just a failure.

Each of us has a tape that runs behind our conscious thoughts in our sub-conscious mind. It is these sub-conscious thoughts that shape our behaviors in respect to whether we pursue our dreams or not because these sub-conscious tapes are what we truly believe about ourselves and about everything and everyone around us. These sub-conscious thoughts control most of our habitual behaviors and routines during the waking hours. An infinite number of different messages could play in your mind. Your experience and your environment deposit these tapes into the sub-conscious, and unless you decide to become aware of them and what they are doing to your behaviors, you could go your entire life not knowing why you react to certain situations the way you do or why you hold certain beliefs about yourself. Below is a short list of negative emotional states and negative personal beliefs that most people carry with them and allow to play unrestrained in their sub-conscious mind:

| | | | | |
|---|---|---|---|---|
| Angry | Failed | Incompetent | Moronic | Skeptical |
| Afraid | Failure | Insecure | Nebulous | Stress |
| Anxious | Fearful | Irritated | Nervous | Stupid |
| Confused | Frustrated | Jealous | Overwhelmed | Unreliable |
| Depressed | Furious | Lethargic | Pain | Uneducated |
| Disappointed | Hate | Listing | Rejected | Unlovable |
| Disgusted | Hurt | Lonely | Sad | Useless |
| Embarrassed | Idiotic | Lost | Scared | Worthless |

Behind each of these negative emotional states and negative personal beliefs stands a ruthless foe that takes no prisoners and kills his enemies at will. This destroyer's name is fear. Fear is not an enemy that you will be able to vanquish easily. In fact, it will take sustained and strategic efforts to retrain your mind to shun fear when it creeps in and to recognize when the fear you are experiencing is healthy or the result of the limiting paradigm. Overcoming fearful states requires you to engage your entire body and mind in a positive and intentional manner because fearful states tend to arrest your entire body and mind.

Let me share a simple example of this principle at work in the life of my oldest daughter when she was six years old. My daughter decided she wanted to learn how to ride a bicycle, so her mother and I took her down to the park to give her lessons on the grass. This accomplished two objectives: a soft crash site and an environment that would require her to peddle as hard as she could. For about an hour we would hold her steady, she would peddle, and then we would let her go. She would ride for about 15 feet and then crash. After an hour of crashing, she began to get discouraged because she could see other children her age riding their bicycles through the park without crashing. Thoughts flashed through her mind that maybe something was wrong with her. I leaned over to encourage her and told her that falling is fine because we never learn to get up until we first fall down to the ground. Part of learning to ride is learning to accept the reality of falling. You must learn to believe in you and to reprogram your thought processes in learning how to deal with the negative and limiting thoughts when they come. I put her back on her bicycle and told her this time she was to say aloud, "I can do it, I can do it, I can do it, I can do it!" while she peddled as hard as she could. The first few times she would say, "I can do it!" but forget to peddle because I was the one pushing her. After pushing her several feet, I would let her go by herself, she would coast, and then crash. Repeatedly we did this exercise. Sometimes she would peddle but not say, "I can do it!" and then crash.

Then it happened. My daughter learned everything she would ever need to know about how to train her mind to believe in herself and overcome negative thinking. I pushed her several feet while she said aloud, "I can do it, I can do it, I can do it!"; she peddled as hard as she could while holding the handlebars straight; and when I let go of her, she was riding her bicycle. I will never forget how five seconds after I let go of the bicycle, her mantra of "I can do it, I can do it, I can do it!" naturally became an audible proclamation of "I'm doing it, I'm doing it, I'm doing it!" Her mother and I cheered as she peddled her feet and rode her bike by herself for the first time. We stayed at that park quite a while as she rode around and practiced her newfound skills. She still wobbled and crashed every so often, but when we left that day, she no longer had to tell herself she could do it because *she had accepted the reality that she could do it.*

Overcoming fearfulness requires us to do things we do not believe we can do. When I first began to write articles and leadership programs, I was scared people would read them and think they were terrible (admittedly, some of them were bad). People wrote to me and called me all sorts of names and attacked my intellect and character. Nevertheless, I kept writing and kept learning. I crashed several times and still crash occasionally. In fact, my first attempt at business crashed, resulting in the loss of my house. My next attempt was successful however the next few attempts after that never got off the ground. Finally, I found success in the building services industry. Then the events of September 11, 2001 compelled me to join the United States Navy. Again, I failed at some things and succeeded in others. Overall, I excelled during my military service, and I am proud of the work I performed during that time.

Each of us has times when we fall off the bicycle. It is fine to fall as long as we learn to get back up again. Eliminate fearfulness by replacing the limiting paradigm with a positive experience that is full of emotion – allow yourself to feel the pride and the excitement of being victorious in something you did not think you could do. Capture that moment in your mind's eye and in your body and recall the sight and feeling of your victory when you are negotiating new experiences that cause the limiting paradigm to tell you that you will fail. This exercise will empower you during times of insecurity and fear.

# THE POSITIVE THINKING HANGOVER - WHERE DISILLUSIONMENT MEETS STUPIDITY

Unsubstantiated positive thinking is akin to dopy optimism. In fact, they are cousins. **Here is the reality**: *sometimes not everything will be all right.* Sometimes there is nothing positive to think about in a situation. Bad things happen in the world all of the time, and nothing positive can come from these events. Sometimes the dice do not roll our way and no amount of thinking positively can change that fact. Sometimes you have to go back to the drawing board and begin again. There has always been a fad in the self-help genre that advocates having faith in the good intentions of the cosmos or in the good intentions of an undefined and nebulous infinite intelligence that will cause everything to align just right in the universe, causing everything to be fine. *That's bullshit.* It is magical thinking. There is no cosmic consciousness looking to help you out while leaving others to starve to death, to be victimized and killed or die in horrific disasters. Bad things happen, and often nothing good can come from these events. The power company shuts off your power if you do not pay the power bill no matter how positive your thinking is. Food will not magically appear in your refrigerator just because you are staying positive and have faith that everything will be all right. People all over the world suffer from hunger every day, and no amount of positive thinking will change that. Children sit hungry in schools in every country around the globe because they have no food to eat for breakfast, and the only meal they will get today is their school lunch. Some children will not even get that much. To say this is because of a cosmological misalignment or prejudice is beyond idiotic.

What fixes this problem is not positive thinking; what will change this situation is positive action and believing that we can overcome the challenge if we work together. Your company will not pick up market share or expand its client base just because all of the senior leadership sit in a boardroom and think positive thoughts about the future. Somebody has to get out there and sell something. Somebody has to fill the orders. Somebody actually has to do the business, and no amount of positive thinking can change the fact that life rewards well thought-out actions. **Period**.

After the promised results of the positive thinking crowd do not materialize, the crushing and disappointing reality is a condition akin to someone who suffers from a hangover. In my meetings, I call it the disillusionment hangover that results from too much exposure to magical thinking. Sadly, sometimes people get lucky a few times, and the dice roll their way, but their luck always runs out. Anyone who has been to Vegas knows that to be true. The house always wins in the end, and so does reality. This short-lived success with the positive thinking crowd has the same effect gambling has on addicts. A few wins sprinkled in with losses keeps the hope alive that you will come out ahead, when the reality is you have fallen into the trap of ineffective positive thinking and have done nothing to get ahead. The harder you work and the more you prepare for success, the "luckier" you will tend to be.

Positive thinking also tends to lower our situational awareness. You cannot fix a problem you are unaware of or deny exists. Remember, you have to face it to replace it. If you have a drinking problem, you have to acknowledge this reality rather than try to convince yourself everything will be just fine. If you have financial difficulties, telling yourself everything will be fine will not make the troubles go away. You have to face the issues head on and have a deeply rooted belief in yourself that you can overcome these challenges.

The winners in life achieve empowerment through knowledge, intelligently thought out plans, and relentless action. Intelligent action empowers people to achieve greatness. Working hard and working smart empower the Quality Paradigm and crush the limiting paradigm. Leave the dopy optimism and positive thinking idiocy to those who are content with only thinking and talking. The only thing that brings contentment to those who have the Quality Paradigm is action that yields positive results. Remember, the world judges you on what you produce, not what you think you can produce.

## CONCLUDING THOUGHTS

The limiting paradigm destroys any chance you may have at succeeding in life. Negative and toxic thinking destroy the best-laid plans. There must be a well-balanced and realistic thinking process in place in order to negotiate difficult and trying times. Not everything along the journey of life will be rosy. In fact, a lot of the journey may be difficult and appear to make the destination not worth the price, but this is only an illusion. We perceive this illusion through the lens of our belief system (beliefs about our environment and ourselves), and the illusion serves humanity as a natural filter, separating those who demand and work hard for the realization of their dreams and those merely content and satisfied with dreaming. Capturing our dreams comes when we pay the price with intelligence, determination, persistence, honor, and character. The Quality Paradigm – leaving everything and everyone in a better condition than how you found them, whenever possible – is the key to bursting through this illusion and achieving your dreams.

Remember, "everything and everyone" includes you. The Quality Paradigm forces you to evaluate what you truly believe about yourself and what tapes you allow to play in your mind concerning your life and your business. The limiting paradigm is full of and perpetuated by negative, toxic tapes that tell you all sorts of lies about the things in your life that are most important to you. There is no way one mind can allow the Quality Paradigm and limiting paradigm to co-exist because they are diametrically opposed and mutually exclusive in every way. Where the limiting paradigm says, "You have failed in the past. Can we really do this?" – the Quality Paradigm says, "We have failed in the past and learned so much. We can do this." The limited paradigm always asks, "Can we?" – while the Quality Paradigm asks, "How can we?" The limiting paradigm says, "You failed." – but the Quality Paradigm says, "You learned; now apply it and succeed."

# PART II –
## A BUSINESS PARADIGM

# PRINCIPLE 3: THE QUALITY PARADIGM AND QUALITY MANAGEMENT IN BUSINESS

*I like pigs. Dogs look up to us. Cats look down on us.*
*Pigs treat us as equals.*

- Winston Churchill

The following chapters are included for the reason of giving some history to the conversation of quality. It is very important for your professional development to have at least a brief understanding of the history behind the most prevalent management philosophies in the Western business models. Admittedly, some of the information in the following two chapters is a bit dry, but the book would be incomplete had this very important information been excluded. The reader would do well to internalize and pay close attention to the finer details of these next two chapters if he or she is in a position to influence his or her company or may desire to be in a position to do so in the future. While the context of the following information is generally from a manufacturing perspective, its principle is widely applicable. I will leave it to the reader to discern the best way to apply these principles within their industry and organizational culture.

## TOTAL QUALITY MANAGEMENT – AN

# OVERVIEW, DEFINITION, AND BRIEF HISTORY OF QUALITY

To understand what the Quality Paradigm is and how it relates directly to your business, we must first understand and define the concept of "quality" in a business environment. While defining quality as something that has definite measurable characteristics would be appropriate in some contexts, this definition falls short of the broader concept that spans across multiple business domains. The difference of products, services, and customer demands forces us to *define* quality differently in every industry from a standards perspective, yet the *concept* of quality always remains the same. Quality is simply ***a product or service that satisfies a person's expectations and needs completely.*** The only way a company can satisfy a customer's expectations and needs completely is to build a Quality Paradigm philosophy into the corporate culture of its business. The only way to satisfy a person's expectations and needs completely is to endeavor genuinely to leave him in a better condition than how you first encountered him.

The Quality Paradigm must become an all-hands and top-to-bottom responsibility. Even internal business elements, which have zero contact with customers, still have an effect on the company corporately and, as a result, indirectly encounters *every* customer. Therefore, we must simplify our *definition* of quality from our *concept*. The generally accepted definition of quality in any industry is ***satisfying expectations.*** The business associate satisfies the expectations of the company for which she works, and the company in turn regards her as one who produces quality work. The marketing manager produces highly effective ad copy, making his company more profitable and therefore produces high quality work. Your quality employees are the employees who produce work to the company's stated expectations and in support of the company's highest priority goals. To produce better results from quality employees, the company needs only to raise the standard of expectation and provide training for the employees to meet that standard. To receive a better answer, one must first ask better questions. To produce a better result, one must first take better action.

Quality control and quality assurance are both parts of a larger more encompassing philosophy called Total Quality

Management (TQM). The idea of Total Quality Management had its genesis in the 1920s and early 1930s. During the boom of the 1940s (due to World War II), pioneers in quality management techniques such as Dr. Joseph Juran, Dr. W. Edwards Deming (from whence the Deming Cycle comes – PDCA), and others broadened the scope and application of TQM processes. The rebuilding of the Japanese economy and infrastructure provided fertile ground for new and better management and production processes. Oddly enough, it was not until some 40 years later that TQM gained any sort of large-scale acceptance in Western countries. During the economic boom of the 1980s (as the U.S. climbed out of recession), companies in the United States tended to be bloated and inefficient, while our Japanese competitors were comparatively lean and very efficient in production and management processes. This made the margins better for our foreign competitors on the business side and produced better products on the quality side. With better quality products priced competitively, it became very difficult for American companies to compete globally. This was especially true in the automotive industry. As the United States headed into another economic recession in the early 1990s and our foreign competitors started to slow down as well, American industry took this as an opportunity to become more efficient, trim down unneeded positions, and re-engineer business practices and processes.

Over the past 25 years, TQM has broadened itself to become applicable to many business domains such as education, health services, military, governmental, and a whole host of industries. TQM is flexible enough to be widely applicable and rigid enough to produce results in just about every industry one could imagine. Many believe that TQM is more than a generic methodology. TQM is a powerful management philosophy that works when senior management invests the time to properly investigate, implement, and commit to practicing for an extended period.

Generally, traditional management, as opposed to TQM, is concerned with maintaining the current system in a functional and efficient state. To illustrate the difference between TQM and traditional leadership and management models, let us examine the analogy of a shepherd watching over his flock. Traditional leaders and managers, or in this case shepherds, keep their sheep (customers) together in one pen, dealing only with the occasional offender who wonders off looking for a better deal. These shepherds seek to lead their sheep from pasture to pasture (transaction to transaction) in an orderly manner. More than likely the shepherds (the business leaders and managers) move their sheep for the same reasons – provisions are becoming scarce or dangerous environmental conditions necessitate a move to "greener pastures."

Often, what drives traditional managers is crisis or immediate needs, and this catalyst creates a "crisis cycle leadership" culture within their organizations that ultimately upsets or scares away all of the sheep. When priorities go out the window, *everything* becomes a hot priority. What follows is unresponsive customer service and dissatisfied customers. The TQM management philosophy teaches the manager and leader to continually look for and move toward greener pastures because *the sheep (customers) like better grass.* The focus has nothing to do with conditions and everything to do with the expectation of the customer. TQM organizations determine priorities by how situations will affect the customer, and the organization adjusts accordingly. To clarify, customer satisfaction in the sense of TQM is not the same as customer service. The customer service aspects of a company may be very good while the product quality is low, and, as a result, customers are disappointed. Thus, the true purpose of the customer service element is to keep that sheep (customer) from wondering off. TQM says the customer should never have to be disappointed with the product in the first place, and the customer service aspect should merely be an extension of the customer experience of total satisfaction.

Traditional managers and TQM managers both seek improvement. The difference is not in the seeking, but rather in the duration of the seeking. As alluded to previously, TQM managers and leaders are continually seeking a better way to serve their customers. This may take the form of better products, better services, better delivery, better customer support, better internal processes, better manufacturing processes, or anything that improves the customer satisfaction. Traditional management addresses improvement from a large project initiative perspective. Generally, it requires the dedication of large amounts of resources to make a big move in the market to capture an opportunity. TQM says resources are continually devoted to small improvement processes directed at what customers are demanding and flow with the market direction continually instead of taking up static residence in one area of the market or another.

Another difference between traditional management and Total Quality Management is that TQM focuses on eliminating waste within every aspect of the organization. Waste can take many different forms, including, but not limited to, raw materials, scrap, over order/production, time, labor, physical space, money, etc. Traditional business considers these costs to be the "cost of doing business." The reality is much different. These costs (waste) are the cost of poor management and a recipe for disaster in today's lean global economy. Truly, these excuses are merely masks for inefficiency and ultimately are the "cost of *going out* of business." Regardless of industry, someone somewhere is designing a system to produce the same product you are producing faster, at a higher quality and grade, with a higher degree of accuracy, and at a lower cost to build. Your survival in your respective market requires you to produce better product, to think clearer, to plan more completely, and to execute more accurately than the next person. The Quality Paradigm can get you there.

## THE FOUR ASPECTS OF THE QUALITY PARADIGM IN BUSINESS

The foundational principle of the Quality Paradigm as applied to business is the philosophy that customer satisfaction and customer loyalty can only be achieved long term through continuous improvement (a philosophy called Kaizen, which we will discuss later). Without a deeply rooted belief in continual improvement, the management of any organization will wonder away from this guiding principle. The natural tendency of many corporations is toward the traditional model; therefore, an ample amount of organizational discipline is required within the ranks of senior-level and mid-level management. The 5S Manufacturing philosophy is an example of how self-discipline (the 5th S) is a virtue that process engineers and management strive to bake into the overall process. Without discipline, it is impossible to keep quality initiatives in place and effective. Loyalty to quality standards and procedures is paramount to the overall success of any quality related philosophy.

## The First Aspect - Commitment to Customer Satisfaction

A commitment to overall customer satisfaction begins with the product or service providing the customer more value than the customer expects. In 1928, Napoleon Hill published a book entitled *The Law of Success*. The ninth law listed in the book is *The Habit of Doing More Than Paid For*. In this law, the author says:

> "The habit of doing more than paid for is one of the most important lessons of the Law of Success course. It will teach you how to take advantage of the Law of Increasing Returns, which will eventually insure you a return in money far out of proportion to the service you render. No one may become a real leader in any walk of life without practicing the habit of doing more work and better work than that for which he is paid."

With few exceptions, many people from all over the world are producing the same work you perform now. Some of these people are performing this work with more accuracy. Some people are offering better features and benefits to their customers. Some people have a better internal business model and thus less overall cost and more net profit. In this global economy, the competition is not going to get smaller or easier to manage. The competition is going to grow, and the market is going to become bloated and overcrowded. The winners are chosen by how much value they provide customers in their overall buying AND using experience. For example, this is especially true in the auto industry. Manufacturers are ever conscious of how the buying experience is almost as important to repeat business as the actually vehicle. The Dealers are also conscious of this principle. Dealers understand that customers who have a terrible or unpleasant buying experience will not purchase their next vehicle from their dealership. However, the converse is true as well. If the customer has a wonderful dealership experience but a terrible experience with the manufacturer's product, the customer will buy a different brand but probably from the same dealer if the dealer happens to sell the brand they are looking to buy. The table below illustrates this point clearly.

| Great Product/Great Experience | Great Product/Poor Experience |
|---|---|
| Result: *Buy the same product from the same source* | Result: *Buy the same product from a different source* |
| Poor Product/Great Experience | Poor Product/Poor Experience |
| Result: *Buy a different product from the same source* | Result: *Buy a different product from a different source* |

This basic principle illustrated here is true in any business, yet I am surprised at how many business people lose sight of this simple idea. When the focus of your business is doing more and better work than the customer expected to pay for, the profits tend to take care of themselves. In an effort to cut costs and boost profitability, businesses have traded this age-old philosophy for one that says it is good business to provide nothing for something. This idea is ridiculous, dishonest, and one of the major reasons so many customers are suspicious of businesses. The behavior of businesses in the past has taught the customer base to mistrust them. Seeking to leave your customers in a better position than they were in when they hired you or purchased your product will not only dazzle your customers but also breed loyalty, breed a good reputation for your brand, and smooth out your financial returns.

The next aspect of the commitment to customer satisfaction is quality. Quality is different from giving the customer more of whatever you are providing than the customer is paying the business to provide. The former speaks directly to bells and whistles and features that give the customer a "Wow!" effect. W. Edwards Deming, an American statistician and quality guru of the 1940s, referred to these features as "delighters." Returning to the automobile example above, each year the auto manufacturers build cars with new "delighters" (features meant to attract customers). This year's options will ultimately become next year's standard features. This cycle is not only endless, but it is universal. All industries have certain opportunities to pack "Wow!" factors into their product, their customer service, their internal function, their delivery, and their sales processes.

Quality does not speak to delighters. Quality speaks to whether or not the delighters are functional. Who cares if the car has four cup-holders, six airbags, and ABS brakes if the engines fall apart at 75,000 miles and the transmission has issues at 60,000 miles? Quality is non-negotiable. Chrysler found this out first hand. Chrysler's inability to produce consistently a quality automobile was above all other issues the main culprit in its decline. The lack of quality in Chrysler products led to distrust from its customers, and ultimately these customers migrated to other brands. An example of a car company that has worked very hard to improve the perception as well as the actual quality of its products is Hyundai. In the late 1990s Hyundai began to see that it would never expand its interests into the Western markets unless they began to build better quality vehicles more Westerners were willing to buy. In a Time Magazine interview in early 2005, Suh Byung Kee, Hyundai's president, said, "When I first came to Hyundai, I, too, didn't think quality cars were important." Clearly, Mr. Kee wised up, took the advice of his Chairman and quality management executives, and began to fund huge quality initiatives that have since brought Hyundai into the mix of quality automobile manufacturers and have made the company a real contender in the global auto industry. This quality push began at the senior management level when Chung Mong Koo, the Chairman of Hyundai, began to push a zero defects initiative and restructured the internal processes of how the company builds cars.

The last aspect of the overall commitment to customer satisfaction is production continuity. All three of these key aspects of building customer satisfaction work in concert to comprise the first aspect of the Quality Paradigm. Continuity in production processes is important because the process of building a quality product (or performing a service) directly affects the customer experience. Processes that are slow and lethargic may produce a quality product but often at a higher cost that ultimately the company passes onto the customer. This high cost directly affects customer experience and creates a dilemma in the mind of the customer who is then forced to ask, "Do I want a good quality widget at $X$ price, or do I want a widget of the same quality at a lower $Y$ price?"

Organizations that find they are hierarchical and change-adverse will also find themselves having difficulty delivering high levels of customer satisfaction. Many companies have "Tin Gods" that appear throughout different divisions within the company, and organizational cooperation and continuity often collapse. Environments such as these have a very difficult time creating products or services with which customers are completely satisfied. The reason is simple; customer satisfaction is not the motivating force for decisions within the organization – politics are.

## *The Second Aspect – Analytics and Evaluation*

The Quality Paradigm requires that all of the processes (for our purposes, a process is a sequence of events whereby inputs undergo transformation into outputs) that directly affect the functionality of the business be monitored to assure they are both necessary and efficient. Monitoring is accomplished through quality assurance (QA) standards, which are written (generally) in the form of SOP's, codes or best practices, and each process is audited periodically against that standard. These audits should tell the senior management whether the process is meeting or exceeding its intended purpose and serve as a real-time snapshot into the functionality of the process.

The senior management should have their fingers on the pulse of the marketplace at all times. In today's global economy, it is imperative that senior-level management employs situational awareness and is keenly aware of where they stand in relation to their customers. Not listening to the voice of the customer or paying attention to what is going on in the internal and external environments of your business are both deadly sins. Avoid them by creating processes to analyze the effectiveness and efficiency of everything essential to your business.

## *The Third Aspect - Human Resource Management*

Quality begins with people. The basic habits, practices, and behaviors of an organization's people will ultimately determine the overall success of that business within their market. Over the years, I have worked with many people on raising capital for many businesses, including a few of my own. These projects can be long and arduous, even painful at times, but necessary. Human capital is just as necessary as financial capital to an organization. Without proper "human funding," quality related projects and programs would fail. I have seen projects fail miserably that were over-funded financially and under-funded on the human resource end. Conversely, I have seen projects succeed that were under-funded financially but had creative, resourceful, and competent leaders in place that got the job done. The difference between first and second place in the marketplace is the quality of your people.

Organizations must bake the Quality Paradigm into the culture of the company from the senior level management to the part-time employee. During my time in the United States Navy, I picked up what we refer to as the zero defects mentality. This meant there was zero tolerance for half-assed work and unprofessional personal conduct. Zero tolerance and zero defects policies breed discipline, *esprit de corps*, and the can-do attitude that takes customer satisfaction seriously. Companies that have employees who believe that "good enough is good enough" will have difficulty reaching their potential in growth and market share. In quality circles, there are few if any grey areas. All that exists is conformant and non-conformant, right and wrong. Years ago, I had a man tell me there was only one way to do anything in the world – *the right way*. His sage advice has saved my career and my reputation more times than I can count. This commitment to do the very best at everything the company endeavors to accomplish and to make no excuses for subpar performance is paramount to long-term success and the very heart of the Quality Paradigm.

## The Fourth Aspect - Continuous Improvement known as Kaizen

Kaizen is more than a fad. Kaizen is a lifestyle and a philosophy. During the push in the 1980s and 1990s to develop better efficiencies in Western business models, Kaizen became a sound bite tossed around at seminars and lectures across the country. Soon after its formal introduction to America in the mid 1980s by Masaaki Imai, companies began Kaizen initiatives in conjunction with Six-Sigma and a host of other quality philosophies. Unfortunately, as the fads began to shift and Wall Street demanded bigger returns, senior level managers began to migrate toward the next best thing in management philosophy hoping to produce better results more quickly. This migration undermined the strength and functionality of Kaizen philosophy for many of these companies. Most of the companies that adhered to the Kaizen philosophy profited handsomely from it. The insightful executives who used the Kaizen philosophy understood that Kaizen requires a *continual* commitment to improvement with no end to the effort. Kaizen is more a state of being than anything else. Day after day, the company is improving and learning. These companies gear all of their processes to capitalize on failure, learn the lessons, re-engineer the process, and move forward.

Leadership from the leadership determines the outcome of any endeavor. Poor leadership above all else is the cause of most failure in life and in business. The same principle employed to provide personal leadership and personal responsibility is the very same principle employed by executives to provide corporate leadership and corporate responsibility. The Quality Paradigm demands the executives, senior management, mid-level management, supervisors, and team leads to be completely committed to perform their jobs with informed leadership. Doing the wrong thing right is still doing the wrong thing. Doing the right things right is what brings success.

A Navy friend of mine used to tell me speed was only helpful if you are going the right direction. The same principle is true in business. Planning and plotting the correct course comes from committed, well-informed leadership. The top of the organization must lead any quality related initiative and implement these initiatives through trainers within the organization to infect the corporate culture with the Quality Paradigm. Then the managers receive the task of maintaining the culture through empowering employees with tools (intellectual and physical) that will make them more efficient and effective at their jobs. When the people improve, the business improves. When the business improves, the products improve. When the products improve, customer satisfaction improves. When customer satisfaction improves, profitability improves. All of this improvement begins with leaders being committed to improving their people in ways that benefit both the company and the individual.

Some 50 years before Kaizen came to America, another man named Walter Shewhart developed what we know now as the PDCA Cycle (known in the 1930s as the Shewhart Cycle and the 1950s as the Deming Wheel or Deming Cycle). The PDCA process operates as a circle and never has an end because the final output becomes the input for the next cycle. The process goes on forever toward continual improvement. For those of you who may not be familiar with the PDCA Cycle, please allow me to summarize the philosophy below:

1. **P** – Plan
    a. In this stage, the manager sets objectives and makes plans based upon information available to the manager at the time.

    b. Many companies (and individuals) get stuck in step one because they are always preparing, always looking for more data, always seeking the perfect conditions to launch a project or making some excuse as to why they cannot pull the trigger now. In business, people call this the *paralysis of analysis*. It is very important that you do not allow yourself or your company to be stuck in step one.

    c. The two basic phases of this step are Problem Identification and Problem Analysis.

2. **D** – Do
    a. This involves Development, Deployment, and Implementation of the plans set in place.

3. **C** – Check/Analyze

    a.   There should be metrics set in place (identified in the "P" step) whereby you can measure the progress, effectiveness, and efficiency of the program or project.

    b.   Analyze the data, and create a plan to correct any defects or inefficiencies.

    c.   If there is achievement of the desired goal, continue toward the next step. If the desired goal is NOT making progress, return to the "P" step, and begin again.

4   **A – Act**
    a.   Implement the processes that need to occur to produce the original plan as a standard process.

## COURAGEOUS LEADERSHIP

Initiating a Quality Paradigm culture is a top-down process. The old saying goes, "As the head goes, so too the body." In Chapter 5 we will discuss leadership in depth; however, I feel strongly the subject should be included here as well. There can be no overstatement as to how important rock-solid leadership is to an organization.

Money and the proverbial "carrot and stick" programs can motivate people for a while, but ultimately highly productive people usually seek something bigger to which to dedicate their lives. They seek to follow leaders larger than themselves, and they seek out new paths of opportunity. The leader's personal level of courage - the courage to make the hard decisions, the courage to enter new markets of opportunity, the courage to shake up the company, and the courage to adapt practices and processes to meet customer expectations is the genesis of this type of leadership. For our purposes here, the definition of courage is feeling fear and moving forward anyway. Leadership requires the company to keep making progress toward the goal of total customer satisfaction and to keep moving forward regardless of setbacks. The courageous leader sees setbacks as set-ups for future success. Setbacks are merely part of the process of moving forward, so keep moving forward.

Below I have listed the eight imperatives of effective leadership that will serve as a boilerplate for leading any sized organization through change or into a TQM driven philosophy. The senior executives who possess the Quality Paradigm are:

1. **Informed:**

   The perception and understanding of the executive concerning his or her company, responsibilities, market conditions, customer needs and desires, and employee issues must *always* mirror reality. If the organization out paces the executive's ability to lead it effectively, the organization will suffer and atrophy; if the disparity is great enough, the organization will fail. A consistent flow of reliable information must be established and utilized to keep up to date with the latest information pertinent to leading the organization. Not only does the executive need correct organizational data, the executive needs relevant and accurate industry data and techniques as well.

   The executive must also be aware of personal bias and expectation within him or herself and within others. Often information can appear in a certain light but upon deeper inspection turn out to be something quite different. This information could well determine a make or break decision the leader is facing. The interrogation of all information is paramount to the leader's perceptions mirroring reality.

2. **Resilient:**

   The very essence of the Quality Paradigm is the characteristic of resilience. Every organization needs both purpose and strategy when setting and achieving its organizational goals. However, goals can be both a blessing and a curse simultaneously. On the one hand, if the goals and strategy are too rigid with no allowance for flexibility due to market change, organizational emergencies, partnership or relationship breakdowns, and the like, the company will be unable to meet the presented challenges or completely miss new opportunities for complete customer satisfaction. Conversely, if the organization has no guiding principles or sense of purposed direction and chooses instead to adapt to every challenge and change in current conditions it becomes impossible to achieve their stated purpose and to provide an experience that "wows" its clients.

Balance is the key to resilience. Resilience requires poise from the executive and confident decisions that flex within an acceptable variance yet do not break. The resilient executive also provides sufficient support for the organization to stay on course and meet challenges with courage. Resilience allows the leader to stay on course while making allowances for unplanned challenges.

3. **Critical Thinkers:**

Probably the most important aspect of successful management is critical thinking. Critical thinking employs logical judgment in decision making based upon the most up to date and accurate data available. Many leaders never learn to think critically about challenges and instead defer to their "gut instincts." While I would never advocate ignoring your gut, I would certainly warn that depending on it solely can get you into a heap of trouble if your gut instinct is wrong. As with resilience, the key to critical thinking is balance between listening to your gut and thoughtfully assessing challenges, verifying information, identifying possible solutions, identifying the probable outcomes of each possible solution, keeping the executive team appraised of the decisions and the rationale for those decisions, and finally taking action.

Good decisions are generally a team sport within the context of a business. Teamwork is paramount to critical thinking at the executive level. The collective experience and business acumen of an executive team is always greater than that of any one executive. There are no "Lone Wolfs" in successful business ventures. Critical thinkers welcome competent people into the decision making process and, by doing so, insure the long-term success of the venture.

4.  **Clear Communicators:**

    The successful executive has mastered the lost art of effective communication and has learned how to motivate the base and the executive team from the inside out. Often inexperienced or poor leaders mistake communication and motivating others for the opportunity to self-aggrandize and narcissistically explain how "if everyone would be more like me" the world would be perfect. Communication must be a two-way street for it to be meaningful and effective. Even when two parties disagree, that does not permit nor does it necessitate the need to be disagreeable. The English word *communication* comes from the Latin word *communis*, which means common or the same. You must communicate clear and accurate information in such a way to insure both the sender and receiver of the information understands the information sent. There are many different types of communication: verbal, non-verbal, tone inflection, body language, etc. Master communicators have learned to employ each of these types of communication in their proper time and to deliver clear and accurate information to another.

    Executives must learn to overcome barriers to the information they are trying to communicate. Some of these barriers are natural, and some of them are self-inflicted. Everything from personal bias, cultural difference, gender difference, experience, inexperience, inattention, and the like all serve as barriers to communicating. If there is a lack of understanding by the organization concerning the Quality Paradigm methodology and what role it plays within the strategy, the organization will not have the opportunity to buy into it.

5. **The Catalyst:**

    As I mentioned before, quality initiatives are a top-down exercise. I cannot stress enough the idea that the strengths and weaknesses of the leaders are reflected manifold throughout the organization. Therefore, the executive must be the positive catalyst for growth and for change. The doors of success swing wide upon the hinges of leadership. The ability to direct and coordinate quality management projects and initiatives is what demonstrates whether the executive has what it takes to lead in the highest levels of an organization. The catalyst does not wait for direction to lead or wait for perfect conditions; he leads from where he stands and plays the cards dealt to him.

    The catalyst is not afraid to make the hard decisions and takes full responsibility for the decisions he does make. The catalyst is decisive and slow to change decisions once made. Demonstrative data is required to make huge changes to a course once set. An effective leader must delegate authority, provide clear and candid feedback to direct reports and superiors, lead from the front, be willing to do what it takes to get projects completed on time and within budget, be open to suggestions, and keep the entire team informed of information imperative to their respective jobs. These traits will build *esprit de corps* among team members and maintain a professional atmosphere capable of producing high-level results.

6. **Confident:**

    Confidence is not narcissism. Confidence is the result of courage and self-respect but no more self-respect than one has rightfully earned. The executive who possesses the quality paradigm must be ready to confidently, respectfully, and aggressively defend his or her position from resistance or an effort to marginalize the project in favor of "how it's always been done before." The executive owes it to him or herself, the organization, the team members, and the project to be candid at all times about a position. Additionally, he or she should be unmovable in his or her conviction unless convinced of better options through the review of better facts. Organizations that encourage leaders to speak around subjects in order to avoid confrontation or to foster a false sense of professional courtesy are asking for trouble. I am not suggesting anyone make rude nor out of place comments, but I am advocating strongly the courage required to have the tough conversations candidly. I am advocating that executives be actively engaged, involved, vigilant, and ready to act by the employment of an ample amount of confidence.

7. **Strategic:**

The strategic leader is the one who has laid out a short term, medium term, long term, and contingency plans. Leaders are thoroughly prepared for logically reasoned risks and potential outcomes. In addition to preparedness, he or she is also the master allocator of resources and human resource management. Exemplifying strategic competency requires laser-like focus, a deep sense of duty, and a willingness to take personal responsibility for both positive and negative outcomes. Project planning requires the determination of many different factors and very thorough due diligence. Executives must receive better answers by first taking care to ask better questions. Knowing what to know and therefore what to ask is paramount to determining the proper strategy for the organization. The apprehension of this sort of wisdom is through experience, education, and most importantly exposure to how business behaves in the world outside of the executive's own company.

After laying the strategy, it is time for the executive to pull the trigger and execute. The best strategies are as effective as no strategy at all when there is no follow through. There are no points in the world of business for good ideas alone. No one ever pays bills in good ideas. People pay bills with money and goods and earn these resources through transforming good ideas into focused action. Once the project has commenced, the executive must monitor the process and make minor mid-course corrections as required to accomplish the project at hand. The executive must maintain control of the project by identifying, analyzing, and correcting or otherwise addressing challenges head-on. Once the project is completed, the executive must analyze all results and processes again for potential improvement to the strategy. Evaluate, evaluate, evaluate. It cannot be stressed enough.

8. **Consistent:**

Consistency is what communicates commitment. The guiding principles that made your company great or that helped to foster greatness within the entrepreneur who has just started a business are the same guiding principles that keep the organization great. When I was new to the devises of business, I learned to see the world in terms of black and red. Morally sound and fiscally responsible business leads you into the black, and corrupt and fiscally irresponsible business leads you to the red (and possibly to jail). The largest key to success in everything you will ever do is consistent performance of morally sound and financially responsible decisions. Consistency has guided me to success in my career, parenting my children, coaching, and interpersonal relationships. Those times in my life when I have been indecisive and inconsistent, I have often met trouble and ultimately failure. In sales, the key to being the best is not hitting homeruns; it is being consistent in closing deals. In management, success requires consistency because consistency produces productive and efficient departments and company operations. In sports the successful players are the ones who produce consistent results week in and week out, not the ones who play well one week and terrible the next. Consistent companies are stable companies; stable companies (generally) are growing companies. The stability of your company is directly and inextricably relatable to the stability and consistency of the executives and management.

# A WORD ABOUT 5S AND SIX-SIGMA

## 5S

5S is the name of a workspace organization methodology that employs a list of five Japanese words (when transliterated into English) that start with the letter S. 5S is a philosophy and a way of organizing and managing the workspace and workflow with the intent to improve efficiency by eliminating wasted material and time, improving production flow, and reducing process variances. The origin of 5S can be traced back to the early twentieth century to two American businessmen who studied the Japanese method of management. While the Japanese did not formally know their method as "5S" in the early twentieth century, they were keenly aware of how to manage effectively their businesses in a lean manner. An American pioneer in the automotive industry, Henry Ford, popularized the method by utilizing it in his manufacturing plants and assembly lines. The Ford "CANDO" Program (Cleaning up, Arranging, Neatness, Discipline, Ongoing improvement) provided the pathway for later generations to develop and utilize what we now know as 5S. Our modern use of the term 5S and the methods utilized today were developed by Hiroyuki Hirano and published in his book *5 Pillars of the Visual Workplace* in 1990 (I highly recommend obtaining and reading this book). These methods went on to revolutionize how manufacturing companies organized and executed production. Often 5S and other manufacturing methodologies worked well (and still do) with Six-Sigma methodologies created and popularized by Motorola in the 1980s. Allow me to introduce briefly the 5S components individually in their manufacturing application:

**Seiri** (整理), or *Sorting*: Removing unneeded objects and materials from your work area and only supplying the workspace with tools and materials required to accomplish daily tasking.

**Seiton** (整頓), or *Straighten or Set in Order*: Efficiency and flow within a workspace. Are components in a logical order or test equipment stored in a convenient space? Are the tools necessary to accomplish tasking in an order that coincides with manufacturing processes?

**Seisō (清掃)**, or *Sweeping, Shining, Cleanliness*: Systematic cleaning to keep the workspace free of debris and clutter.

**Seiketsu (清潔)**, or *Standardizing*: To maintain control over processes and easily spot variations in manufacturing process (or the process of delivering a service). This also creates a standard against which we may measure quantifiable results and staves off the natural tendency of the law of diminishing returns.

**Shitsuke (躾)**, or *Self-discipline*: Maintaining and reviewing standards of the quality program to insure the processes are still meeting demand and are functioning properly. Discipline will guard against reversion in methodologies to *"how it's always been done in the past."*

### Six-Sigma

In former GE CEO Jack Welch's 2005 book entitled *Winning*, he articulates masterfully in very precise terms what a complex statistical process such as Six-Sigma really means to an organization on a macro-level:

> Six-Sigma is a quality program that, when all is said and done, improves your customers' experience, lowers your costs and builds better leaders. Six-Sigma accomplishes that by reducing waste and inefficiency and by designing a company's products and internal processes so that customers get what they want, when they want it and when you promised it.

Simply put, Six-Sigma removes variance from repeatable processes, and this lack of variance creates less waste and non-conformances as a result. I would encourage anyone who is interested in learning more about the subject of Six-Sigma or *Lean* Six-Sigma to research one of the many companies who offer high quality certification training.

## QUALITY CONTROL VERSUS QUALITY ASSURANCE

Finally, before we tackle continuous improvement, it would be helpful to define and discuss quality control (QC), quality assurance (QA), and highlight their differences. Too often managers see quality control and quality assurance as one in the same. They are not the same. Quality control and quality assurance work together in a symbiotic relationship to produce a whole quality program. Quality control is concerned primarily with executing processes and techniques that fulfill quality standards and produce a conformant result. Quality assurance is concerned with analyzing results, improving processes and techniques, and making sure these all work together properly to produce their intended product.

To highlight further the differences between quality control and quality assurance let us discuss the typical steps in each problem management process. During the quality control portion of the problem management cycle, the management process will typically include:

1. **Problem Identification:** With the discovery of a problem (non-conformance), it immediately enters the problem management cycle and undergoes analysis. This assumes your organization has already created systems to manage properly non-conformities. If this prerequisite system is not available, the problem identification step will ignite a new crisis management cycle because the situation forces the organization to be reactive instead of proactive or responsive.

2. **Problem Analysis:** Often the employment of the five whys root-cause analysis process (or some other RCA process, for example: fishbone, fault tree, or change analysis) determines the cause of a non-conformance or under-performing production line. During the analysis phase the production element (manufacturing) should:
   a. Define the non-conformance or problem,

   b. Gather data (evidence or failure or non-conformity).

   c. Ask why (up to 5 times if necessary) and identify commonalities between the evidence and the defined problem.

   d.   Identify the root cause.

3.   **Problem Correction:** Once the suspected root cause has been isolated:
   a.   Adjust the processes to delete the cause of the non-conformity. As a word of caution, verify that this change will not cause new errors in a different part of the production process. This is achieved through cross checking functions, inputs/outputs, and interfaces between departments.

   b.   Engage new processes.

   c.   Analyze implemented changes to verify effectiveness.

   d.   Repeat if necessary and document,

The output from the quality control process becomes the input for the quality assurance element. The typical problem management cycle for quality assurance includes:

1.   **Data Gathering:** After sending inputs from the manufacturing or maintenance side of the equation, the process of gathering as much information about the non-conformant product begins. The QA element investigates all of the data and organizes it into a quantifiable form. Generally, this form is numbers, ratios, and percentages.

2.   **Trends Analysis:** QA analyzes the information for trends. The company can utilize this trend information to forecast defect ratios, determine inspection rates, and a whole host of other uses as deemed necessary by the management.

3.   **Process Identification:** This stage of the process generally deals with specific aspects of the total production process. Most production processes utilize many subsystems (or sub-processes) to comprise a

larger singular system (or process). Identifying which subsystem is faulty or may have a tendency to fail is foundational to resolving and preventing further non-conformity. Risk management begins with identifying potential hazards.

4. **Process Analysis:** After QA identifies the faulty process, it analyzes the process to ascertain why it failed and to reconfigure, repair, or replace the process as needed. Then QA forwards this information to the proper level of management, and they make the decision as to how to amend the process.

5. **Process Improvement:** The process improvement phase is a collaborative effort (generally) with the production side of the business. Often the engineers, production managers, and QA managers are involved in the creation or repair of the process in question. The rule of thumb here is that *over* communication is better than *under* communication. The key here is clear, concise, and deliberate correspondence. When doubts or questions arise, *address them.*

## CONCLUDING THOUGHTS

The intention of the information contained in this chapter was to acquaint you with quality control and quality assurance ideas and philosophies as well as introduce you to the general characteristics and strategies that will help you climb to the top of your organization and stay there. While it may ruffle some intellectual and academic feathers, I believe deeply that no amount of education can take the place of or offer the value of investing time – sometimes years – in the trenches learning business first-hand. Nothing can replace the successful experience of a grizzled veteran executive when the chips are down and the going gets tough. Contrary to some, I believe old dogs can learn new tricks. Effective veteran executives understand the value of learning and intellectual self-investment. They ask the hard questions of themselves before they ask them of others, and they immediately fill in any deficiencies in understanding critical to their success.

If you are new to business or possibly have just started a small business, you have a steep learning curve ahead of you. The good news is there are plenty of great resources, such as this book, to help shine the light on the dark roads that lay ahead. In addition, I would recommend the S.C.O.R.E. Program offered by the Small Business Administration (www.score.org) for just about any type of business advice. SCORE was founded in 1964 and has provided counseling to over 8.5 million business owners, including me. SCORE counselors are at the heart of many successful business ventures and many small businesses that have eventually become very big businesses, such as Vermont Teddy Bear, Vera Bradley Designs, and Jelly Belly Candies. For more information directly associated with quality and quality assurance, I would recommend you contact the American Society for Quality (ASQ – www.asq.org) and dig deep into tools and resources they have available. If quality assurance is your job, I would encourage you to find an association such as ASQ and become involved with other quality assurance professionals in your industry and in your area. These people are a wealth of information for the new quality professional to experienced veteran.

# PRINCIPLE 4: CONTINUOUS IMPROVEMENT

*He who stops being better stops being good.*

- Oliver Cromwell

Over the past century, revolutions in technology have driven American innovation. Our advancements have largely come because of great leaps forward followed by plateau (and many times decline) and then often out of sheer necessity another revolutionary leap. Since the rebuilding of Japan in the 1940s and 1950s, the Japanese have taken an entirely different approach to progress and change management. Instead of revolution, they chose to follow the path of *evolution*. This evolutionary philosophy of progress is more harmonious with nature and the tempo of everyday living. Each day things change. Today is not like yesterday, and tomorrow will not be like today even if the change is not apparent. Everything in the universe is hurling forward at breakneck speeds in a constantly changing motion. Even if we desired to stop the constant change in the world around us (and many people do), the feat would prove impossible. Life and business demand we find *its* tempo and begin to dance with change and make situations work for us.

Many speakers and trainers sell "solutions" to the problem of finding the proper tempo of life to well meaning, but often desperate, business and sales people and aspiring entrepreneurs.

As a result, all sorts of strange philosophies have come and gone through the business and motivational genres over the years. For me, what is stranger still is that so many otherwise intelligent people flock to these ideas so readily. These ideas are wildly popular with the aspiring businessperson or leader because they generally leave out two key ingredients – sustained effort and self-discipline. The concepts these gurus preach are often simple restatements of principles that have been around for ages. Nevertheless, there is a big difference between simple principles and easy execution. Just because something is simple does not mean it is easy. For example, the principles for winning in business and in life are simple enough but certainly not easy to execute. If these principles were easy to execute, many more people would be successful in their endeavors. Success takes effort over time.

Kaizen is about sustained effort. Life is not about the big wins, and neither is Kaizen. Sure, we all experience big wins now and again, but waiting for the next big win will most often leave you in the poor house in the mean time. Revolution is about instant dynamic change driven by necessity and passion. Most of the time revolutions fail to achieve lasting change, and when they do finally fail, there is usually blood on the floor, and often people get hurt. Evolution is about small, consistent, and sustained changes over a given period of time and in concert with the environment or greater context in which it finds itself. Nature and everything within our known world is subject to the forces of change through the process of evolution. Your business is also subject to these same shaping forces whether you are aware of them or not. The Japanese Kaizen philosophy is the fundamental business philosophy that breaks the revolutionary cycle that drives "up/down" results. Kaizen picks a point in the future and implements a sustained strategy of minor changes until achieving the desired improvement.

Not everyone is accepting of the idea of continuous improvement because it requires change. I have found people are good with change unless of course it affects them. Many business leaders become defensive and openly hostile to anyone who challenges, however well meaning, professional, and respectful, the corporate philosophy that drives their corporate culture. Often businesses hire professionals, specialists, and consultants to make improvements and to help facilitate a change management project only to be met with open resistance every step of the way by the very same executives who hired the professionals in the first place. Comparatively, this is like going to the doctor to find out what is wrong with you and cussing him out when he gives you the diagnosis and the prescription. To say this is madness is to state the obvious, but it must be said because it happens every day in companies all over the world. Do not let this happen in your company. If conditions are going to improve for your business or in the least, stay on a profitable course, everything must be on the table to be evaluated, and everyone who has a stake in the survival of your business (read: every employee) should have an opportunity to make suggested changes about *anything*. In fact, suggestions should be required from every employee.

If the principles you hold as the guiding light are indeed as great as you say they are, then surely the principles will be substantive enough to withstand a critical inspection of how it adds value and helps to facilitate the overall strategy of your organization. As a business leader, you must be secure enough in your foundation and guiding principles to welcome and lead the charge in evaluating what is truly driving your business. Attacking consultants and well-meaning employees does nothing but kill morale, discourage creativity, and lower individual (and thus collective) production. Many of the companies who are growing are the companies who ask for improvement ideas from every person in the organization and have no subjects that are off limits to critical inspection. These companies believe deeply that quality is everyone's responsibility, and they back up that belief by empowering their employees to suggest and make approved changes. If you are in a position to take a poll of your employees, ask them how they would solve the most pressing issues your company is now facing. The assembly line worker can probably give you a good look at where inefficiencies lie in your processes. The business staffer can tell you how to process financial reports and claims more efficiently. I guarantee you will be amazed at the things your employees see that can greatly benefit your company. But (you knew there would be a "but"), you have to have the courage to ask and more importantly *the courage to listen.*

J. Paul Getty, the American industrialist, once said, "I'd rather have 1% of the effort of 100 men than 100% of my own effort." This very interesting principle is also true in business and process improvements. Kaizen philosophy says that it is easier to manage and control small 1% improvements over a long period of time than it is to manufacture and manage huge revolutionary change when conditions and clients demand it. Satisfying customer desires *does not* mean performing revolutionary feats of incredible engineering, marketing, and manufacturing to meet market demand. Many businesses are late to the party when addressing customer expectation because they do not have a system to listen for the voice of the customer and predict where market demand is heading. Instead, most companies react to the market shift and miss opportunities to gain market share. When you listen to the customer, you can make small improvements each day to properly address common problems inherent to doing business, the needs of your clients, and meeting those needs as they demand them. The effective manager will quit thinking about business and life in terms of huge events and start thinking about life and business in terms of fluid progress toward improvement. Life is not static. Life is fluid. Business is not static. Business is also fluid. If your business is to survive, it must get in the flow and *evolve*.

## A SHORT BACKGROUND ON KAIZEN

The principle of progressive improvements is not new and not indigenous to the Japanese culture. We find the same ideas from every corner of the globe (yes, I am aware globes do not have corners) and from the times of antiquity. However, the systematic philosophy of Kaizen as we know it now has its roots in the 1940s and 1950s post-war rebuilding efforts of Japan. As quality awareness increased in Japan after the war, Japanese manufacturers and businessmen began to study the methods of American industrialists like Ford. In particular, the Japanese were interested in how Ford and others during World War II had made it possible to produce 18 to 24 fully functional B-24 Liberator bombers *per day* in the Willow Run bomber plant. This amazing feat of manufacturing helped to assure the allied victory in both the Atlantic and Pacific theaters of war. When the Willow Run bomber plant finally stopped producing planes for the war, it had produced an amazing 8,685 *fully functional bombers* from

1941 to 1945 for the United States Government. Ford and his team of engineers had done the impossible through studying and utilizing lean manufacturing techniques. (Though these techniques were not known as *"lean,"* their techniques were lean for their time. The term *"lean"* was not used until 1990 in the book *The Machine That Changed the World*, by James Womak.)

As Japanese industrialists searched for better ways to produce their goods, two aspiring Japanese executives who worked for the Toyota Motor Company studied Ford's techniques and processes and began to apply them to their manufacturing system. These executives, Taichii Ohno and Shigeo Shingo, turned the Toyota Motor Company manufacturing process into what would be destined to become the Toyota Production System (TPS) and in the process revolutionized how every manufacturer in the world would come to view production. Central to this new system was a philosophy of constant improvements made in small incremental movements known now as Kaizen, the Japanese word that means "continuous improvement" or "good change."

While the Japanese wholly embraced the role of lean manufacturing and structured processes, they roundly rejected the coercive management philosophies of their American counterparts. The coercive and brash style of early American industrialists was not compatible to the Japanese culture that chose instead to tap into the potential of each of their employees. The Japanese model excluded no one from becoming a solution to problems within the manufacturing and quality processes. Simultaneous to their move to empower employees, Ohno and Shingo worked to shorten production lines and remove unnecessary space in the production systems. They incorporated suggestions from employees and lineman, broke the American model into smaller pieces, and made them more efficient. Where the American system had been long and rigid, the Japanese system had become shorter and more flexible. This allowed the Japanese to accomplish something Ford had not been able to do: produce multiple products on one line. This innovation would ultimately propel the Japanese to be able to produce goods and services at a rate with which their American counterparts could not keep up.

Soon the tide would change, and American companies began

to send executives and consultants to Japan to learn how they were able to produce goods and services at such an amazing rate and high quality. To their folly, the American executives who studied the Japanese processes tried to emulate the methods without duplicating the culture. Many businesses make this mistake. If your company's leadership is unaware of process context when trying to duplicate and implement new processes, they will usually face tough times ahead. Process, context, and culture must always fit together like a hand into a glove. If your company utilizes a great process that will work when implemented and the context from which it came is comparable to your own but the culture is not compatible with the proposed new systems, it may be time for a culture change. **Never allow your corporate culture to hinder your corporate maturation process.** There comes a point when your company needs to mature in its behaviors and interpersonal conduct. There comes a time when your business has to grow up.

Every company faces a season where conditions force it to grow up and put away processes, practices, and cultures that will not sustain them in the future. There is no cookbook or recipe for producing goods and services. Your company must find its own way to incorporate new methods and processes into a corporate culture that embraces growth and is never satisfied with the status quo or execution that is "good enough." Good enough is never good enough when you have the capability to execute at a higher caliber. There is no way to duplicate a process without first creating the right cultural environment to sustain the new methodology. If this means creating a paradigm shift throughout the organization, then you may need to think about initiating a change management project to get your team where it needs to be culturally before initiating new sweeping process changes.

## THE BENEFITS OF KAIZEN

When utilizing Kaizen in the context of a quality improvement initiative, the positive impacts are generally immediate and very effective. As with any quality initiative, Kaizen is a top-down exercise, and as the leader, you have to buy into the program and lead from the front. Planning and implementing Kaizen is not a matter you should delegate to mid-level management and observe from afar; if you are the senior leader, you have to actually get your hands dirty and lead the effort. The three big benefits of Kaizen (and there are many more than three) are: a reduction in waste, which directly benefits the profitability and efficiency of the organization: improved asset utilization, which maximizes assets of all types: and as mentioned above, provides immediate and measurable results, which builds organizational momentum.

## WASTE (*MUDA*) REDUCTION AND ELIMINATION

The aim of Kaizen initiatives is to reduce waste. If you are having efficiency or waste issues in inventory, process-waiting times, worker actions, employee competency, over/under production, or any other aspect of your company, the solution to reducing or altogether eliminating the waste is Kaizen. In Kaizen circles waste is called *Muda*, and *Muda* is subdivided into the seven main culprits of waste: overproduction, unnecessary transportation, inventory, unneeded motion, defects, over-processing, and waiting between processes.

### *Overproduction*

Overproduction destroys profits, and it may lead to excess inventory, more chances for defects, exposure to over-processing, and increased waiting times due to the volume of work or system overload. Eliminating overproduction means you produce only the products you need at the time that you require them. In the Toyota Production System (TPS), the achievement of eliminating overproduction is through a process called Just in Time (JIT) production. It is the result of meticulously timed process schedules and highly accurate production processes.

Most companies do not have the processes in place or the trust in their existing systems to achieve JIT production cycles. Most companies strive for a "Just in Case" production system driven by the idea that it is better to be safe than sorry. The mere fact that they feel this way reveals that the company most likely has quality issues they are either unaware of but believe could exist or are aware of but have no idea how to correct. Their reasoning tells them is it is better to have too many products produced and to be able to meet increased demand by digging into inventories than it is to walk a thin line and run the risk of production or quality issues and fall behind.

When the production of high quality products through highly accurate manufacturing processes drives the company's paradigm and cultures, the fear of quality or production problems goes away *because there is trust in the system*. Kaizen improves the manufacturing processes to the degree that less and less overproduction is required to meet market demand while increasing the overall quality of the products. The employment of forecasting demand and planning for growth over a set period also aids in producing what you need when you need it and results in almost zero overproduction and less inventory.

## Unnecessary Transportation

Unnecessary transportation increases production costs because it increases the risk of product damage due to unnecessary handling, increases the costs of labor by requiring excess material handlers, and increases time between processes moving products from one stage to another. Process mapping and production flows that shrink the physical space between production stages will reduce the need for unnecessary handling, excess material handlers, and the risk of damage moving the products between stages.

Ironically, the major pushback for not retooling or reorganizing production processes to eliminate these inefficiencies is often profitability *despite* the inefficiencies. Reorganization brings the risk that the effort and resources invested in the retooling may yield nominal or no measurable improvement and disrupt functional systems. In addition, the company will have to create an atmosphere of buy-in with all of the employees involved in the reorganization. When companies weigh the risk against the benefit, many times they do not see the value added to reorganization to warrant such broad changes. Ultimately, fear of change drives the decision to be safe rather than sorry. This sort of thinking is the reason many companies stagnate because it permeates every decision they make. Kaizen would recommend small process changes over an extended period in an effort to work towards the ideal production process and involve all of the employees into the solution process by asking for input and ideas on how to shrink the space between production processes.

Several years ago, I worked with a company who implemented this Kaizen approach over a five-year period and eliminated the need for an entire production location by consolidating every stage of their production and quality assurance processes to two locations instead of three. The third location was reduced to a servicing center to meet the needs of large clients in the area, but the bulk of overall production was completely consolidated elsewhere. The move cut overhead and all associated production costs by millions of dollars ahead of the economic collapse of 2008. Leaning out processes *ahead of* an economic crisis versus leaning out processes *because of* an economic crisis is much easier to manage because you have the latitude to dictate the terms of the process change.

## Inventory

Inventory costs your business capital, increases overhead costs, increases exposure to damage or loss, and eats up valuable resources such as space and time. Please be aware of the fact that not all inventories are bad. Businesses need certain inventory for daily functioning. The inventory Kaizen targets is unnecessary inventory that will not be used within an immediate window. Holding inventory that has no demand attached to it would constitute unnecessary inventory because the company does not know how long they are going to have to store it (which means the associated storage costs are uncertain). Unknown variables make it difficult to project costs beyond estimation. Kaizen cuts most of the unknowns out of the process and only holds the required inventory for a specific time and use in the future. The storage costs become certain, and the business can create a forecast of all associated costs.

## Wasted Motion

On the surface, wasted motion may not seem to be a big concern; however, wasted motion in respect to essential tasks contributes to inefficient production. Just because a worker is moving does not mean he or she is working efficiently because there is a distinct difference between motions and work – work being any motion that directly results in the production of goods or services. Kaizen works to eliminate wasted motion and leave only motion resulting in work. The movements of the individual must always correlate to the accomplishment of work. If the movement is unnecessary, there is the opportunity for increased efficiency.

For example, if a production attendant has to walk back and forth a total of 500 ft between stages to complete one cycle of a task and he or she is expected to produce 12 cycles per day, the attendant will walk over one mile per day. This is one mile of wasted motion that does not directly contribute to the production of products per day. Annually, this worker will have walked 240 to 250 miles! Assuming it takes the worker about 2 to 3 minutes to make one whole trip, each year the worker will have wasted between 96 and 100 hours just walking between stages and producing *nothing*. That is between 12 and 12.5 workdays each year simply walking! Translating that into dollars wasted, the figure can become a tidy sum of money before you realize it. Assuming your worker has a wage of $20 per hour, the wasted money will be between $1,900 and $2,000 per employee at a minimum. Moreover, the company exposes itself to any risk to the well-being of the worker if he or she has to walk past any sort of equipment or production area where a mishap could occur. Safety related injuries and the resulting time off and medical expenses cost companies millions of dollars each year. Additionally, as if these exposures were not enough, companies also expose themselves to unnecessary legal action when workers are hurt on the job due to a function that was the product of wasted motion.

Wasted motion is very insidious and often overlooked. There must be training for management and team leaders to keep a watchful eye on this form of waste, identify it when they spot it, and immediately work to eliminate it while maintaining production quantity and quality.

## Defects

Arguably, one of the most expensive of the seven wastes is the cost associated with defective or non-conformant products or services. Processes such as Six-Sigma are specifically designed to address the elimination of defects on a basis of defects *per million*!

The defects rate breakdown in the chart below indicates how many defects per million opportunities a company can expect if it operates on a 1 to 6-Sigma efficiency rate.

| Sigma Level | Defects Per Million Opportunities | Percentage Defective | Percentage Conformant |
| --- | --- | --- | --- |
| 1 | 691,462 | 69% | 31% |
| 2 | 308,538 | 31% | 69% |
| 3 | 66,807 | 6.7% | 93.3% |
| 4 | 6,210 | 0.62% | 99.38% |
| 5 | 233 | 0.023% | 99.977% |
| 6 | 3.4 | 0.00034% | 99.99966% |

For the sake of illustration and at the risk of over-simplification, let us suppose for a moment that each defective product results in a total cost, including labor, of $20 per unit. If your business is operating at a 2-Sigma level, defects and rework will cost your company over $6 million. If you compare the cost of rework at a 6-Sigma level company, it would only be only $68! This purposely over-simplified example should clearly highlight the power of doing the right things right the first time. Kaizen employs methodologies such as Six-Sigma (among many others) to work toward eliminating virtually all defective products and to keep these low defect rates consistently over an extended period.

## *Improper Processing*

Companies who overkill and over think how to accomplish tasks usually cause improper processing during the entire production phase. Process overkill is like buying a 747 for the free peanuts. Overkill is the buzzword involved with this form of waste. Many times companies upgrade to technology and equipment that are expensive to purchase and expensive to maintain when the equipment they currently use is capable of producing the same level of quality products. Toyota Motor Company is a primary example of a company that produces high quality products utilizing older equipment that is well maintained and utilized efficiently along with well-planned automation.

In the spirit of doing the right things right, Kaizen eliminates waste in the "doing the right things" part of the process. Kaizen and the methods directly involved with manufacturing set-up and process flows seek to eliminate wasted resources on processes and equipment that do not add the appropriate amount of value to the quality of the product. In order to justify an upgrade in equipment or process, there must be a directly associated cost/benefit. Businesses should not expend capital for a new piece of equipment, software or process unless a cost/benefit analysis clearly demonstrates the value if they will add the product. If there is not benefit that is directly attributable to a capital expense, then there is no justification for the capital expense. **Bottom line**: *Do not spend money on items that do not add value and that do not reduce waste to your company.*

## Waiting

We have come to the waste that happens to be my pet peeve: waiting. Waiting occurs most often because material and information flows are poor, the formation of process points are in improper proximities, and often these points are then not syncopated properly to produce the products at the time the next process needs them. Your processes must be set in such a way that no waiting (or minimal waiting) results from the process before it or after it. When processes fail to have proper syncopation or have improper automation, it slows or stops the continuous flow of goods, and waiting is always the result. Waiting takes the form of unproductive gaps in the overall production rate of a business. Eliminating these gaps will greatly increase profitability as well as worker output. Timing and flow are the key words to be concerned with when working to eliminate waiting periods.

People who fail to meet deadlines cause another source of waiting. Not only is this unprofessional, but it is amateurish and indicates a lack of professional competence required to work in management or leadership of any kind. Missing a deadline is as unprofessional as being late to an appointment or to work. Not to mention, missing deadlines affects everyone in the process, and it tells your colleagues that their time is not valuable to you. This is one of the ultimate acts of professional selfishness committed in a business setting (not to mention a personal setting). If you miss a company deadline and, as a result, the company loses a day of productivity, that day of wasted time is a day the company can never get back, and they may come to you looking for remuneration in the form of your employment. When I was the supervisor of my shop in the Navy, the first rule I told the new sailors upon arrival was "do not be late *for* anything or *on* anything." For emphasis, the second and third rules were also "do not be late *for* anything or *on* anything." The fourth rule was "if you are going to be late for anything or on anything you had better call and give me some lead time before your scheduled deadline." Causing others to wait for projects, products, documents, information, or any other materials creates wasted time at every subsequent step in the production process. If delays are unavoidable, you must communicate this information to all parties involved.

If you are engaged in the selling of personal services or a service-based industry, do not ever be late for any meeting with a client, potential client, or colleague from your own firm or another firm without having a damn good reason and making them aware of the situation with enough lead time so they can re-adjust their schedules. An hour of wasted time costs people money. For example, if a professional's income dictates he or she is worth $200 an hour for a standard eight-hour workday and you decided to be late 15 minutes without a phone call, you just cost this person $50. If he or she is subsequently late for their next three meetings, you have just cost three other people money as well. High-income earners are aware of facts like these. Do yourself and your reputation a favor, and never be late for anything except a cocktail party for which it is appropriate to arrive fashionably late.

## ELIMINATING ABSURD (*MURI*) PROCESSES

When dealing with any effort to eliminate *Muri* there are two major factors (among many details) you must consider:

1. **Is this process engineered properly?** How does this process make sense in producing a product or service in the leanest manner possible? Can this process be reduced further while maintaining quality standards and not overwhelm operators?
2. **Is this process resourced properly?** Do we have the manpower to meet current and increased demand, and do our production layouts create unnecessary steps within our process that slow work and overwhelm our workers?

Before we discuss absurd processes, I must disclose the other proper and popular translations of *Muri*, which include "overburden" and "unreasonable" and which we will discuss further. However, after many years of dealing with process set-up and training I make it a point to define *Muri* first as "absurd" because of the epic inability of many companies to reduce concepts and processes to their lowest denominator. When I run across a process that does not make sense or is inefficient, I will ask my client, "How does this make sense?" Forcing managers to justify processes is a healthy habit to get into if you are a senior manager. Many times what makes sense at one level does not make sense in the larger scope of the business. This is another example of why the top of the organization needs to drive quality initiatives. While I am sure a few exceptions exist (though I am aware of none) bottom-up quality initiatives do not work long term and often result in chaos and strife because front line employees do not have the responsibility (even though they may have the desire), the authority, or the resources to make the change meaningful and lasting.

I have found that many times companies are keenly aware of how absurd some of their processes are, but due to familiarity and habit, they eventually learn to live with the inefficiency and work around it. Another reason companies learn to live with absurd processes is that even when made aware of the absurdities the executive leadership fails to address the process and in so doing gives their implied consent to continue the practices. What follows is the idea from employees and management that "if it does not bother my boss why should it bother me?" The *status quo* ensues, and then another cycle of absurdities begins. Eliminating absurdities is very important because your product quality and efficiencies are directly tied to your processes.

Kaizen philosophy works to reduce processes to their lowest denominator by standardizing work using several small working groups along the process flow. Instead of one or two long working groups in a process, Kaizen breaks the processes into "bite-sized" steps and then reconstitutes them into one full process. The standardization of work in each work group produces standardized outputs from each step in the production process. Hence standardized inputs flow into each successive step within the larger process. This allows for increased flexibility and accountability for quality checks.

Please understand that the application of the Toyota Production System (TPS) to manufacturing can be very involved and complicated even after all of the absurdities have been wrung out of the process. Many highly competent certified consultants in manufacturing process engineering and management are available to help your company to negotiate these obstacles. A good place to start looking for a consultant to help guide your business through this process is the American Society for Quality (ASQ).

Over-burdening and unreasonable (from the standpoint of workload) processes are not necessarily absurd processes because, while the process may over-burden workers, the cause may not be the process; the process itself may be sound, but the demand on those processes may be excessive. The root cause of a dilemma like that may be as simple as proper resourcing and checking work efficiency of individuals along the line. Possibly, the process may be fine, but the flow of the process on the floor may require reordering, or the proper tools may need to be set closer to the individuals on the line. Maybe the growth rate of the company has increased the demand on the process and stretched the output capacity to the point of diminishing quality in the final product. The distinction between absurd and over-burdening processes is that absurdity generally deals with the processes that have not be engineered or organized properly and reduced to their simplest forms, and over-burdening processes usually deal with resource and demand issues placed upon those processes. When your company is working to eliminate the waste of *Muri*, be aware that both of these issues, absurdity and over-burdening, must be considered and addressed in turn.

## ELIMINATING INCONSISTENCY (*MURA*)

Have you ever met someone who had erratic mood swings and never exhibited an even temperament? This person needed to have *Mura* eliminated from his or her personality. In business settings, the elimination of *Mura* seeks to address up/down output fluctuations and bring evenness to each step thus bringing evenness to the entire production process. For example, if your process has five steps and steps two and five are working at a fevered pitch while steps one, three, and four are working at a normal to slow pace, you have a problem with process unevenness. Steps two and five will always lag behind the other processes, while often times the other processes have to wait (waiting is one of the seven wastes of *Muda*), which creates wasted time and inefficiency. Another product of inconsistency is over-production and inventory along with their associated costs. I am sure you have noticed all of these waste categories have an interconnection with one another in some way. When setting up internal processes for your business, it is very important to take special care and ample time to consider the processes you are going to utilize to produce your goods or services.

Additionally, you should also carefully consider the most efficient method of facilitating the internal processes of the business. Producing products or services efficiently but not being able to manage human resources, accounts receivable, accounts payable, and the sales departments also contributes to waste. Bringing overall evenness and consistency to the entire organization should be included in your overarching strategic plan. Be mindful that many managers are not familiar with lean thinking and lean principles, so looking to bring in a specialist may be a good solution for your business if you are realigning business processes. Another solution may be to facilitate a series of seminars to train leaders and managers in lean thinking and methodology.

The goal with training is not to make them quality experts but to make them aware of quality methodology and the rationale used to make decisions in a Kaizen culture. If you are just starting a business or if you have a small business that is starting to expand, you may seek to employ a specialist to give you counsel and direction for setting up your internal processes. You can find these types of people by contacting a retired executive through the S.C.O.R.E. Program offered through the Small Business Administration. You can find the contact details for the program at the end of the book in the resources section. Of course, I am always able to assist you in any training project you are thinking about initiating.

Inconsistency can take many forms and affect many different

aspects of your business. In the opening example above, I asked if you knew of any individuals with erratic mood swings who lived in a cycle of unevenness. Following that example, I would like to discuss the importance of how a person's overall personal demeanor affects everyone around them. In the interest of full disclosure, I will be the first to admit that I have an intense, hard charging, and very candid personality. I believe deeply in working very hard, and I believe in equally playing very hard. My ability to focus on getting things done and moving onto the next task is very important to me and, from my perspective, is at the core of my successes in life. Those times I have met with defeat, the root cause was often a lack of focus and not being certain of what I wanted out of a situation. Consequentially, my personality has been known to run people over inadvertently (ok, sometimes it is intended) resulting in a situation where I have to go and make amends. That said, I try very hard to have a pleasing and otherwise agreeable personality.

Parenting two daughters with two completely different personalities has taught me patience and flexibility in dealing with others. They have both taught me kindness and gentleness. In general, parenting has taught me to regulate my emotions and to be consistent in my responses and decision-making. I am very thankful to have had the opportunity to be a father and to learn how to move from being a father to being a dad.

Another place this lesson was taught to me was volunteering for an organization that fed and clothed the homeless and provided assistance to the addicted and abused. I had the opportunity to lead a wonderful group of volunteers in facilitating the services we provided for the community. Leading by inspiration and employing a pleasing personality is essential when working in a volunteer environment and this experience helped me to cultivate both of these traits. You must learn the same lessons in leading your organization or your department. Anyone with the proper training and qualifications can get a job as the leader, but it takes a special person to be the kind of leader who others want to follow.

Some biographers say the great industrialist Andrew Carnegie would not tolerate a man who had a disagreeable personality and those who refused to work in harmony with others. The great author and businessperson Dale Carnegie believed the same principle as well. The value of positive energy and *esprit de corps* within a company is beyond measure and the leaders and managers must model it first. An inconsistent and disagreeable personality will destroy the productivity of a company and lead to many different forms of waste including human resources turnover. Organizations must eliminate personal *Mura* among leaders and managers in the same way they eliminate it from processes.

## CONCLUDING THOUGHTS

The Kaizen philosophy has catapulted countless organizations to the top of their respective markets and revitalized otherwise flat or declining businesses from the graveyard of failed ventures. Resurrecting businesses and careers is possible only when the paradigm of continuous improvement is not only embraced but also espoused. Revolution may serve as an initial catalyst for change but ultimately is a long shot when utilized as a tool for creating lasting or permanent change. Conversely, the principle of evolution over time followed by intense persistence and self-discipline develops corporate and personal habits that make change permanent and sustainable.

You can find the principles outlined in this chapter (and many others) in the Toyota Production System (TPS). It was not my intent to expound on the finer details of TPS. Many fine books are available that can give you a systematic blueprint on formulating and implementing a TPS program within your organization. I have included many of these in the resources section found in the back of this book. My aim with this chapter was to introduce you to the general ideas found within a Kaizen ideology and to show you practical ways you can apply this philosophy to your business and to your life and eliminate waste, absurd processes, and inconsistency.

# PRINCIPLE 5: LEADERSHIP

*The supreme quality for leadership is unquestionably integrity. Without it, no real success is possible, no matter whether it is on a section gang, a football field, in an army, or in an office.*

- Dwight D. Eisenhower

When deciding on the final contents of this book, I hesitated on including a chapter on leadership because of the volume of books and information produced about the subject each year. People are obsessed with leaders, leadership, and performance enhancement. There are management and leadership gurus who ebb and flow with the latest leadership fads. People produce books and programs making fantastic claims of unbelievable results for clients who utilized their systems and programs. It seems the market for leadership material can never be too full. But even with all of the mass of information at society's fingertips, leaders still fail and find ruin. Companies hit the rocks of bankruptcy or fall into disrepair each year. There seems to be no end in sight to the leadership crisis occurring in halls of government, corporate boardrooms, educational classrooms, and homes all over the world.

I decided to write this chapter because somewhere along the way it has become acceptable to provide quick fix, minimum effort options, and require top dollar. *Somewhere along the way, good enough became good enough, and we lost our sense of personal quality.* The entitlement culture of our current age is only a symptom of the deeper criminal mentality that tells people they are entitled to something for nothing or maximum benefit for minimum investment. The idea of "leverage" has been prostituted and polluted by social engineers, crony capitalists, and public officials to boost profits, please shareholders, placate constituents, and enrich the social, business, and political elites. Our financial institutions have sold customers down the river and created organizational processes that benefit no one but shareholders and executives. Companies intentionally gear their manufacturing processes to provide the lowest quality product acceptable to maintain market share and then boost prices to the customer. Service providers and contractors cut corners to lower internal costs but demand prompt payment at top dollar for half-assed workmanship. This mentality corrupts even our colleges of higher learning and academic circles. People thought to be credible academics pass off outright lies and pseudoscience to enrich the few for the sole purpose of selling snake oil solutions to the world and enriching themselves and their cohorts in the process. Where will this madness end?

What happened to doing ethical business? What happened to providing more than required and going the extra mile for clients and customers? Who redefined the term "value" to mean the least for the most instead of the most for the least? The companies who will compete for industry dominance in the future will be those who marry the sound principles of ethics with the sound business practices that brought many businesses to the forefront of the global economy a generation ago. The principles that made companies great in ages past are the same principles that can make any company great in the twenty-first century. Individuals need to raise their standards of personal accountability and leadership if we are to outlive the sins of our past. Institutions, organizations, and governments will only realize lasting change when people who have the courage say loudly, *"Good enough is no longer good enough, and we want excellence."* When the *status quo* is no longer acceptable, things will begin to change. I have hope for our collective futures. The winds of change are beginning to blow around the world. There is an air of discontent with empty suits making empty promises and shysters promising the rain, but delivering only the clouds. The international struggle against extremism and growing intolerance for impotent and corrupt leadership is beginning to see the sprouts of springtime. Nevertheless, there is still much work to do if we are to move beyond past sins and indiscretions. The Quality Paradigm is the cornerstone of hope upon which we can found future business relationships and mutual good will.

## LEADING FROM THE INSIDE OUT

Like so many people these days, I did not come from a storybook home. Many of my childhood experiences created emotional and intellectual baggage that caused me serious problems early in my adulthood and in my career. I suffered from the complex that nothing I produced was good enough to please people. I constantly desired acceptance from others, and this need for acceptance caused me to act in ways that were not an expression of who I really was on the inside. Looking back, I cannot pinpoint an event or single moment when I realized I had lost myself, but over time I realized I had become a conglomeration of who people wanted me to be at the expense of who I wanted to be, and I was absolutely miserable. My desire to do my best and to produce good work was authentic, but I was not being authentic in how I led myself and how I related to others. I found that people would follow my lead (primarily due to my strong personality and charisma) for a while but then suddenly leave for no apparent reason. In the beginning, I took this personally and could not figure out why people would just up and leave or distance themselves from me.

One afternoon during conversation about this problem, my friend and mentor, the late Derill Cannon, told me in his uniquely dry and direct manner, "It's because people know you're full of shit. They see you lead with your head, but your heart ain't in your decisions. You think you're making good decisions, and most of the time you do, but they know *you don't know you're making good decisions. You think more than you know.*" My initial reaction was one of shock and insult, but deep down I knew he was right. The truth, no matter how painful, often has a certain tone that resonates within us. If you are not authentic with your team, they will never have the confidence to follow your leadership long term. The meaning of authenticity and commitment is having something invested. Being authentic signals to others that you are "all in" concerning your role and that you are willing to put personal stock into the success or failure of your business. It does not matter how well you make decisions if your inability to be authentic prevents people from trusting you.

When I joined the Navy, I learned how to shed the façade of being what other people wanted me to be and to be myself. This newfound authenticity coupled with my knowledge and skill in business and leadership allowed me to fly through the enlisted ranks from E-1 to E-5 in a little over 3 years. While I would love to tell you that learning to be authentic and less guarded will cause everyone to suddenly open up and love you, that is certainly *not* the case; in fact, quite the opposite. Many of the people who liked who you pretended to be will dislike who you really are; some may even attack you verbally or professionally. Conversely, people who would have avoided you in the past will be more open to your ideas and to your leadership and management. It is a core truth of personal leadership: **preferring people to dislike you for who you are is better than people accepting you for who you are not.** You have to learn to be good with that last sentence. If you cannot find the courage to learn this lesson, you will face painful relationships the rest of your life. This idea really sits at the very core of your ability or inability to lead you and by extension to lead others. Authenticity breeds respect, and respect is the essential ingredient to personal power with others.

Everyone has problems. Everyone has issues and needs to improve in their relationships, finances, businesses, or a whole host of other things. Denial of problems and weaknesses never leads to a position of personal strength. Remember, you have to face it to replace it. This principle is true at every level and in every situation. Seeing where "the baby is ugly" begins with asking hard questions about yourself; your goals; your past, present, and future; your current financial or professional situations; and your actual responsibilities versus your perceived responsibilities. Some of the questions you need to ask yourself are:

1. Am I lazy? Have I set the bar too low for myself and expected too little?
2. Am I fearful? Have I set the bar too high so I will have an excuse not to succeed?
3. Do I lie to myself by promising to do things but not

follow through with any or very few of them? Could this be part of the reason I have little respect for my word and myself?

4. Do I avoid personal accountability for my job and delegate work I know is clearly within the realm of my responsibility? Could this be why my area of responsibility is constantly off-track or in a continuous cycle of catch-up?

5. Am I intolerant, greedy, narcissistic, overly insecure, or cowardly? You may be tempted to dismiss all of these with a quick glance, but that would be a mistake. These negative emotions and personal states will assassinate any attempt you make to succeed in life or begin leading from the inside out.

   a. **Intolerance** clouds the mind and disavows any ideas other than its own. The intolerant mind is quite small indeed. It takes a mind open to new ideas and being a positive influence on those fellow travelers working through the journey of life to find success and personal fulfillment. I grew up in a very intolerant home, and consequently I became very intolerant as well. I readily admit this dragon does escape from its cage on occasion, but I am ever mindful of its potential to destroy the peace and satisfaction I work hard to create in my life and encourage you to see areas of your life where intolerance rules the day and ruins your experiences. These will be the areas in your life that can realize the greatest growth potential.

   b. **Greed** is generally rooted in fear and/or an overly ambitious ego. Many men and women have come and gone who have gathered at the expense and often in spite of others. Greed is not a sickness that effects only the wealthy. In fact, many of the greediest and most hateful individuals I have ever met are poor. They think constantly about what they can gather from others at no expense of their own and what society owes to them. Greed is the criminal mentality that expects of others, takes at the expense of everyone and everything around, and then provides no value in return.

Some may argue that capitalism is rooted in greed, but I would disagree. Capitalism provides opportunity to men and women to provide bountifully for their fellow man while painting the masterpiece of their life with the brush of action. Crony capitalism is the real villain of all humanity of which we should be aware. This is the type of system that enriches the powerful, provides no opportunity for anyone else to profit or to prosper, and provides little or no value in return for its cost. Much of American business has fallen victim to the deception of thinking that the only thing that matters in this world is the bottom line.

Look with a close eye at your expectations. Do you want something for nothing? Is the value you offer proportional to the remuneration you demand?

c. In my humble opinion, **narcissism** is the most unbearable of this list because self-importance is the product of immaturity and delusion. I was once subject to a terrible punishment when the company I was working for at the time forced me to sit through monthly meetings led by someone who for courtesy's sake we will call Rebecca. She was slender women, not overly attractive, but extremely outgoing. The company awarded her a high position simply because of family relation. Rebecca was neither competent, business savvy, nor intelligent yet because of inheritance was extraordinarily wealthy. In these monthly meetings, Rebecca blathered on about how difficult it was growing up poor, but with hard work and commitment (neither of which she had invested) one day we all could be just like her - *successful*. By the end of these "motivational" talks, most of us wanted to either kill Rebecca or shoot ourselves. Apparently, she never got the memo that the prospect of becoming a half-assed copy of someone else is not motivational, nor is it a good definition of success by most people's estimation. These facts only served to highlight for the audience how completely out of touch with reality this person was.

The lesson here is if you have placed a value on yourself higher than what you deserve, you need to get over yourself; you are not that awesome. None of us is.

d. The preceding state is generally a cover for being **overly insecure.** All of us are insecure about something. Men and women obsess about different things, but both are rooted in a discomfort within themselves. A monologue (called self-talk) plays repeatedly in people's minds telling them that they are not sufficient in some way. Often the monologue plays unconsciously and will only grow loud enough to be heard consciously when situations require the demonstration of action. People come to believe over the course of time (from childhood onward) that something is inherently wrong with them. Often, the culprit here is religion, culture, or family upbringing.

The monologues people allow to play in their minds tell them they are:

too tall
too short
too fat
too skinny
too blonde
too brunette
too dumb
too lazy
too inexperienced
too scared
too disabled
from the wrong side of the tracks
too male
too female
too Black
too White
too Native
too Mexican
too conservative

too liberal
too independent
too gay
too straight
not gay enough
not straight enough
not born in the right part of the country
raised in a bad situation
trapped by past sins
too married
too divorced
saddled with too many kids
working too much
not working enough

All of these monologues push us to break our second ground rule: **No excuses**. Do any of these monologues or variations thereof play in your head on a daily basis? If they do, they are keeping you from being your authentic self and following after your goals. I am not advocating the idea that everyone has the potential to be a millionaire, a famous actor, a professional athlete, a top producing leader, or the world's best friend. What I am saying is that everyone has the potential to be the best version of themselves by pushing the limits of their personal best, banishing irrational insecurities, and making a commitment to improve just a little bit every day. Is the person who stared back at you in the mirror this morning a better, more competent, and more able person than the one who stared back at you yesterday? If you answered anything but yes to that question, you have work to do on your personal development. This leads me to ask: if you are not confident that you are improving every day, how can you be confident your company is improving every day? The simple answer: *it cannot improve until you improve.*

e. **Cowardice** is a harsh term. I chose the word cowardice over fearfulness because there are some instances when fear is justified and the proper emotion to exhibit. This is not so with cowardice. Cowardice is the cruelest master of the five negative states that I have listed here (and there are many more, some of which we discussed in Chapter 2). My definition of cowardice is a lack of courage when courage is required. Courage is feeling fear even to the point of fright but taking action despite the fear because the situation or condition demands you do so.

In the military, police departments, and all emergency services, men and women are trained to carry out their duties for the benefit of their fellow man in the face of grave danger and often times insurmountable odds. Consistently, these warriors and homegrown heroes shock us with their bravery and acts of supreme valor, and yet too often they humbly reply that they only did what others would have done in the same situation or simply did what their training required them to do. Herein lays the key to overcoming the professional cowardice that plagues so many businesspeople today. We have educated our leaders and our managers to perform the mundane everyday duties of their jobs and failed to train them in how to make the tough decisions that affect the lives of people around them. We have failed to train them in developing the mental toughness to have the hard conversations and face difficult tasks with honor and dignity. Professional cowardice is due in large part to a lack of consistent and persistent training.

Professional courage is a trait you must learn through repetition. I remember the first time I had the task of terminating an individual's employment. It was the week of Christmas 1999. Our company had won a large job with a very large vendor in the area. Our company bid this particular job in such a way that there was little room for error, but the deal was still profitable. The supervisor (who had always performed his job well in the past) I placed to manage the job mismanaged his time and material resources. This resulted in huge cost overruns in labor and materials, and the job was finished late. To make matters worse, the supervisor walked off the job to attend to personal business and left unqualified workers at the job site unsupervised. The situation forced me to go down to the job site and finish the job myself in the middle of the night. Once the job was finished and the client was finally satisfied, our profitable deal had become a financial alligator. The owner of the company was furious and demanded I fire the supervisor immediately. While I was mad with the situation, I was not inclined to fire someone the week of Christmas and could not bring myself to do it. To avoid a confrontation, I planned to let him go after the New Year's holiday. The next day when the owner came into the office, he asked me if I had let the man go yet. I replied that I had not and told him my plan to let him go after the first of the year. Figuring him to be a compassionate man, I thought he would agree with my reasoning and think better of firing the supervisor the week of Christmas – I thought wrong.

The owner leaned across my desk with one finger pointed at my nose, and in a very stern tone told me in no uncertain terms (and with several expletives) that if I did not fire that gentleman before noon he was going to fire me and then call him in and fire him too! This happened around 8:30 AM. I let the supervisor go two hours later.

If you think it was easy, it was not. *The man cried* and kept begging me to give him another chance, but I had to refuse and ask him to turn in his keys and company tools. The owner of the company taught me a very important lesson that day; it takes courage to perform your tasks even when faced with emotionally or physically difficult decisions that may cause an uncomfortable conflict. Over the course of the two years I led this business, I fired several people for a variety of different things. I learned how to make the hard calls by training and repetition.

Then a few years later, I learned professional courage in a deeper way from the United States Navy. The United States Navy and Marine Corps hold the core values of Honor, Courage, and Commitment. To the Marine or Sailor courage means:

- To meet the demands of our profession and the mission when it is hazardous, demanding, or otherwise difficult
- To make decisions in the best interest of the Navy and the nation, without regard to personal consequences
- To meet all challenges while adhering to a higher standard of personal conduct and decency
- To be loyal to our nation, ensuring the resources entrusted to us are used in an honest, careful, and efficient way
- To have the moral and mental strength to do what is right, even in the face of personal or professional adversity

> Do you exhibit this sort of courage when executing your responsibilities in your personal and professional life? Are you this committed to making the right decisions and taking the right course of action despite the consequences to yourself simply because it is the right thing to do and the honorable course of action? What if the definition of courage listed above was the definition of courage your company espoused itself to and aspired to demonstrate? What would happen to the morale, performance, and profitability of your organization? What would happen to the overall character of all of your staff and colleagues?

## LEADING FROM THE FRONT

There is no secret to leading from the front. Leading from the front is leading by example. Whether you like it or not, or whether you are even aware of it, you already lead from the front. Therefore, the question is not "Do I lead from the front or not?" The question is *"How well* do I lead from the front?" Leading from the front is unavoidable. Even if you hide in your office and bark orders through a speakerphone, you are still leading from the front, and that style of leadership will have negative consequences. Throughout the course of this book, I have spoken many times about the word *consequences* because there is no other word more important to the success or failure of a leader. Other people in your company notice everything you do or fail to do. Everything has consequences. Some consequences are positive, and some are negative, but all are the result of the action or inaction you have taken. Every consequence is the result of leading from the front because that is the position of a leader – in the front.

Sitting down when there are tasks to be completed and challenges to overcome results in accomplishing nothing. The business will not run itself. The reason you are the manager or leader is that it is your job to manage or lead. You should not be there for the sole purpose of a paycheck. If the only reason you do your job is for the pay, your leadership will lack passion and the selfless determination it takes to exhibit inspired leadership. There are many opportunities to learn and grow in every situation. Learning leadership is an ongoing process with no arrival date. I look forward to moving forward each and every day learning new aspects of leadership, reading new ideas about management and organizational growth, and speaking with other business and academic leaders who are at various places along the same path of leadership I travel. Often my children hear me joke about living to be 120 years old, but I must admit I am only half joking. No matter how many years I am alive, I plan to *live* each one. The foundation of living is learning. If your employees and staff do not feel your passion and see your commitment to learn and to grow personally, they will never believe your plans to grow organizationally, and they will rarely perform to their peak potential.

Leading by example means the routine things you perform should be automatic. If you or your business is struggling to cover the basic operating tasks of your business, it is time to wise up and focus on the fundamentals of doing good business. Over the years, I have seen business after business sabotage themselves by missing the fundamentals of doing good solid business. Many large corporations fall into the trap of over sophistication (or unnecessary sophistication), and they get away from doing the routine "Business 101" principles correctly. A primary example of this occurred in 2008 when Lehman Brothers and Bear Stearns collapsed due to gross overextension and *basic* mismanagement of investments. Not to oversimplify the debacle, but the fundamental reason the companies failed was because they were greedy, and this greed influenced them away from executing basic principles properly.

Another example of the importance of executing the routine tasks properly is the National Football League 2009 NFC Championship game between the Minnesota Vikings and the New Orleans Saints. The Minnesota Vikings out played the Saints *in every single statistical category*. Clearly, the Vikings were the better team and played a better overall game. The one category the Minnesota Vikings failed to control was turnovers. They turned the ball over to the Saints five times to the Saints one turnover. The Minnesota Vikings failed to execute the most basic part of playing football – holding onto the ball. This failure to execute on the routine things cost the team a trip to the Superbowl and propelled a team who appeared to be clearly beaten into the national championship.

Years ago, I owned a real estate investment business. Each time my company purchased a property or performed a due diligence evaluation we framed every investment as a separate project and utilized basic age-old investment techniques and leveraging percentages to make sure we were never caught in a bad spot. If an opportunity did not fall within our standards of an acceptable risk, we by-passed the opportunity or passed the opportunity to a firm that was better suited to capitalize on the investment potential of the property. Early on in our formation process, we made a very clear business decision to take every opportunity as a separate deal and to make sure to properly construct each individual deal. The company philosophy believed that if we took care of the details in all of our individual deals, the larger picture would take care of itself and overall control over the strategy, and balance of the company would be easier. Today, I use this same philosophy when dealing with personal financial decisions, investment decisions, as well as personnel decisions, strategic planning decisions, and just about any business related decision you could think of.

**The little things matter; they always determine the big things.** Many times small business owners and entrepreneurs believe that when their company grows to a certain size they will be able to focus more on the big picture issues. This is only a half-truth. If the small things are missed due to mismanagement while your focus is on big picture issues, it will not matter whether you are making sound decisions at that level or not, the minutia will undermine momentum, and like a levy whose foundations falter, an unchallenged flood of problems will pour in.

Currently, the world is in dire financial straits because somewhere someone failed to follow principled leadership concerning their duties. They failed to learn and apply the Quality Paradigm. Certainly, there is not just one someone; there are millions of someones internationally who failed to act prudently.

There are countless examples of this truth demonstrated in just about every area of life. Bad habits and behavioral patterns are communicable. This principle includes financial management. What would happen if we modeled the positive principles of financial management and fiscal responsibility for our children and their children? What if we taught them to invest in their own future by saving and investing a portion of their income before paying anyone or anything else? What if they learned to be patient and to be mindful of over spending? What if they learned to purchase appreciable assets and to avoid financing depreciable assets? Would this affect the future of our governments and of the safety and prosperity of people all over the world? I predict it would transform the world as we know it within one generation, but transformations like these take place only when leaders lead in principled directions driven by a strong ethical code to do the people's business properly.

## KICKING ASS AND TAKING NAMES - THE POWER OF ATTITUDE

Kicking ass and taking names is another way of saying that quitting is never an option. People who kick ass and take names are ready to attack life with energy, a supreme confidence, and an optimistically realistic outlook that seems to propel them over or through obstacles that would have stopped other people in their tracks. People who kick ass and take names energize themselves and energize others around them. There is no substitute for the presence of this type of an attitude inside a team setting.

The upper-level management of your company should have a supremely positive mental attitude and a never-say-die mentality about accomplishing the work at hand. The Quality Paradigm is an element of creating this energy and positive atmosphere that expects success and charges forward even when faced with difficult or unforeseen challenges.

Confident people have an internal monologue that they have learned to control. This monologue tells them they can achieve anything they set their mind to accomplish. This is the seat of their confidence. Several different things shape the monologue, but generally, environment and experience are the main ingredients. A person's past and present environments and experiences most often shape how they view themselves, others, and the world around them. Often it also shapes how they desire to see their own future. If this view is negative, the future can feel like one long repeat of the painful past, and hopelessness sets in. If this view is positive, the world will appear full of opportunity to change the painful past into a promising future.

Let me share another story from my experience in the United States Navy that highlights the kick ass and take names attitude that compels people to never-say-die. As I have mentioned before, my primary job when I joined the Navy was that of a Naval Aircrewman. At that time, in order to earn the right to fly in the Navy as an enlisted sailor, you had to complete Naval Aircrew Candidates School in Pensacola, Florida. A large portion of our training was water survival skills, which would not have been a problem had I not been afraid of the water (I know what you are thinking – why did I join the Navy if you are afraid of the water?). After passing all of my survival tests, I had one last test to complete – the one-mile swim in 80 minutes or less. Honestly, I did not think I could do it. How is that for positive mental attitude?

Treading, floating, and swimming underwater are one thing, but swimming an entire mile was something entirely different. Fear gripped me as the days drew closer. I remember one evening very near the day I was to complete my swim, I was able to see my family. My girls were so excited that daddy would be completing this school and be coming home soon. What my daughters did not know was if I failed the swim test, I would not be coming home until I did pass, or worse, the Navy might completely drop me from the program. Being dropped from a special program often meant being sent to the fleet undesignated (having no set job), which ultimately meant I would be painting the ship haze grey and doing all of the grunt work it takes to successfully operate a naval vessel. Many times a man's pride can be his ally, and this was one of those times in my life. There was no way I was going to come home and tell my daughters I had failed, let alone go to the fleet undesignated to paint the ship haze grey.

The day came when we were to swim our mile. I was so nervous I felt sick, but I had a kick ass and take names attitude that burned deep inside and told me no matter what happened in that pool I was going to swim until I either drowned or finished the mile. The whistle blew, and we all jumped into the pool and began swimming. I used the breaststroke and found a rhythm. After about thirty minutes, people began to finish. I was not even half done, *but I kept swimming.* Then 40 minutes came and went, and more people finished. Then 60 minutes came and went. At the 70-minute mark, my instructor yelled at me to get moving because time was short. I was the last person in the pool at this point. Other people were already showered and in their uniform. The bleachers shook with my fellow sailors hollering at me and cheering me on. I struggled and flailed. My body was so exhausted it was numb. After 75 minutes went by my instructor told me I was almost there, but I had to hurry or I would not make it. With every ounce of energy I had left, I swam as hard as I could. Finally, at 78 minutes and 55 seconds, I crossed the line and finished. My instructor yelled, "You got a hell-of-a-lot of heart kid! Good job."

I relay this story not as a boastful example of my success but as a reminder that even though you may be afraid, even though you may not think you can do this or that, even though you feel that you are weak and cannot go on, if you have a kick ass and take names attitude of supreme confidence and an intense desire to never quit, you can succeed. I was not the first sailor out of the pool that day. I was not even the second or third. *I was the last person out of the pool that did not fail.* **Nevertheless, I did not fail.**

A year later when I put those gold aircrew wings on my chest for the first time, I remembered my defining moment in that pool.

Though I was dead last in the pool that day, I gave 100% and earned the right to stand tall as a Naval Aircrewman. I did not fail because I did not quit on myself, on my family, or on my Navy. On that March afternoon, I got out of the pool and collapsed from exhaustion, but I got out knowing I would never have to pass that way again because I had heart.

### How's your heart feeling?

Over the course of the past fifteen or so years I have read, listened, or watched hundreds of materials on the effects of attitude on performance. Sadly, I must report many of these programs are nonsense. They present a false hope, a false motivation, or more frequently a half-truth laden carrot at the end of the proverbial stick so people will buy the next book or attend the next seminar. It would be irresponsible of me to lump all of these sorts of materials in the same category because there is a broad spectrum of quality among these types of motivational products. However, there is absolutely no doubt that the disposition and mental state of a person's attitude is one factor among many that can determine the trajectory of a person's experience. The battle of the mind is truly the battle for your true self – the core of who you really are.

However, this is only part of the larger picture and a fraction of the many forces at play. Often, people who take success and personal development from a one-dimensional perspective focus all of their attention on creating a positive mental state and consequently fall into the trap of the "paralysis of analyses." These people can tell you one hundred different ways to be positive and display a positive attitude about their own lives yet cannot figure out how to translate that knowledge into action. None of their positive thinking ever enables them to overcome the fear that keeps them paralyzed. From there, a time of justification (read: excuses) sets in and finally the *rigor mortis* of the satisfaction of simply knowing what to do finishes them off. You will find them stuck in the same situations, same relationships, same addictions, same struggles, and same careers completely satisfied that they know how to change everything they do not want to experience in their lives, but they never pull the trigger and execute. The problem is that there is no catalyst that propels them forward to purposed action guided by laser-like focus. The wheels just spin, and eventually dissatisfaction mounts once again. Remember the principle: **Once there is "buy-in," there has to be applyin'.**

Attitude is a part of the equation for success, but it is not the only part of the equation. Thus far, we have spent an ample amount of time on the importance of taking action on strategic plans. In this discussion on the importance of attitude, I want to make sure you do not lose sight of the necessity for action. Life rewards action, and it aligns attitudes. Successful people have an energy and sense of confidence that draws people of like purposes into alignment with well thought out plans. I am a naturalist, and do not believe in the metaphysical mumbo jumbo of cosmic alignment and situations of destiny. I believe people make their own destiny; however, I must admit that a strange thing occurs when you decide on exactly what you want out of life, develop and exude the energy and self-confidence to obtain it, and are engaged in working toward that end. It seems that several individuals will suddenly appear in your life who possess similar goals, well-developed skill sets, and a desire to join you in your pursuits. Sometimes it is you who is drawn to someone with a plan and who is taking action to achieve a goal larger than any one person is.

Belief and positive attitude are not expressions of arrogance; they are expressions of supreme confidence. As consulting expert Dr. Alan Weiss says, "If you don't toot your own horn, there won't be any music." By that statement, Dr. Weiss does not mean to promote an arrogant demeanor but rather a supreme confidence that is unafraid to express what value you can provide for your clients or employer. A person must have a certain swagger about them; a hop in his step that is different from the normal person you would meet on any given day. Confidence has no pretension or *prima donna* element involved and no need for self-aggrandizement. Often confidence is quiet and thoughtfully spoken in terms of intelligent discourse and well thought out positions. Confidence at times is also assertive and constructed of principled material.

Too often people who are confident and have a certain presence that fills a room suffer the accusation of being arrogant or self-centered when the reality is much different. Over the years, I have heard many people be unfairly critical of confident, driven people. Sadly, this is often due to a naturally occurring reaction of personal insecurity and only highlights for listeners how immature the speaker truly is. These types of people often resort to *ad hominem* arguments and personal criticisms because they have no way to refute the substance of the other person's position. If you are the recipient of these types of attacks, the best policy is to ignore the personal attack the best you can and stay on message and stay positive. The world is a very harsh place, and many people will line up to stop you from achieving your goals. Not everyone is going to like you, and you have to learn to be okay with that reality. I would bet you do not like everyone you have ever met or encountered, so why would you expect or even hope everyone would like you? Get over it. There are no silver bullet personality types that everyone likes and that no one dislikes. Confident people do not waste time majoring on the minors or try to win company popularity contests.

In Victor Frankl's seminal work *Man's Search for Meaning,* he relates the experiences he endured while a prisoner at Nazi Germany's Theresienstadt and Auschwitz concentration camps. During World War II, Frankl lost his parents and his wife to the Nazis as well as endured terrible experiences of imprisonment. After his liberation in 1945, the only remaining family Victor Frankl had left was one sister. Through all of these terrible experiences, Frankl maintained that life has meaning, even our suffering and negative experiences. Frankl is quoted as saying, "Between stimulus and response there is a space. In that space is our power to choose our response. In our response lies our growth and freedom." Victor Frankl learned that there is no profit in ignoring reality; the profit lay in looking at conditions from a different perspective and assigning it the meaning you desire for it to have. Things are bad because we consider them bad. While obviously situations and conditions can be favorable or unfavorable in relation to your goals, how you view the situations and conditions is entirely up to you. You determine your response. Ultimately, you determine the color of your experience.

## CONCLUDING THOUGHTS

Leadership requires many things beyond the scope of this chapter. In no way am I trying to produce any sort of exhaustive discussion of the subject, nor am I trying to oversimplify the matter either. The three ideas captured here are the three areas I have observed that otherwise thoughtful and competent leaders miss most often. These are simple things really: being authentic by leading with your true self, making sure you take care of the fundamentals each and every day, and developing an optimistically realistic attitude about life and work. Those three principles will transform a person's experience if he or she will thoughtfully apply them to different areas of his or her personal and professional lives.

An interesting fact I hope is not lost on you is the positive effects of a positive mental attitude on the health of an individual. In a February 2008 article for ABC News, Dr. Charles Raison, who at that time was the director of Behavioral Immunology Program at Emory University School of Medicine, related the following:

> "It is very clear from research that's emerging that in general, a positive mental attitude is in fact a huge protector: A. against feeling unhappy when one is stressed out; but may also protect people from the physical damages that occur in the body as a result of stress. And this is probably because what a positive attitude does is it allows us to perceive stressful situations in ways that seem less threatening or less dangerous. And when that happens, our brain doesn't tell our body to activate all these stress and inflammatory pathways that damage health. So yes, there's a lot of evidence that a positive outlook is in fact good for health.

> The only caveat to that is there are some studies suggesting that if people have unrealistically positive attitudes and then reality doesn't live up to those expectations, sometimes people can then flip the other direction and become overly pessimistic -- so there's a little bit of a caution there. But in general, realistic positive attitude is one of the best things we can do for our health."

Developing an attitude that allows you to approach life and work with a can-do, kick ass and take names attitude will improve not only your performance and job satisfaction, but it will have positive effects on your physical health as well. It will also allow you to open up and become more authentic in your leadership. I like the caution that Dr. Raison leaves the reader at the end of his statement. He inserts the sobering ingredient of realism. As stated before, in no way am I advocating flighty, pie in the sky positive mental thinking tricks. There is no way you can just think positively, speak positively, and be positive and magic money bags will fall out of the sky. Life does not work that way (though there are many who would like you to believe that it does – for a nice fee, of course). That sort of ideology is simply bullshit and borders on lunacy. There is a difference between positive beliefs and stupid beliefs. Being overly optimistic is as dangerous as being overly pessimistic. The balance to leading well and having a kick ass and take names attitude is to be optimistically realistic. If you can look at your life and your company, see where the baby is ugly, be honest about what the root causes are, and be positive that with hard work, smart leadership, and patience any challenge can be overcome, life will be a whole lot easier, not to mention more enjoyable.

# PRINCIPLE 6: COMPETENCE

*If you don't keep score, you're only practicing.*

- Vince Lombardi

There are few, if any, conditions more crippling to a company or organization than leaders and managers who *know what to do*, but do not have the competency to deliver. Incompetent leaders and managers will not only slow down internal processes, but they will frustrate the competent people who work for them. Many times, I have seen leaders try to point to past successes, academic accolades, or reputation to supplement or otherwise excuse areas of incompetence. Here is the reality: nobody cares what you produced *last year*, if you are unable to produce **this year**. Nobody cares what college you went to or what degrees you have if the results you produce are less than competent. Nobody cares who you think you are, who your business card says that you are, or how great the press reports that you are *if you fail to deliver promised results*. People always want to know, "What have you done for me lately?" Lately, meaning *today*. No matter how passionate you approach your work or your life, if you fail to deliver results, you will be regarded as a cloud without rain. There is no replacement for competence. There are no replacements for hard work and focused efforts that yield valuable returns. The mere perception of competence and results never paid a single bill. Competence, execution, and results pay the bills. Holding the office is not enough – **you have to do the job; you have to perform.**

Personal competence drives organizational competence, and organizational competence is every bit as important as individual competence. Your company is only as competent as the people who work for the company. In addition to individual competence, companies have to account for process competence.

Many times companies will have an amazing line up of talented and competent individuals, but the corporate policies in place that are supposed to facilitate the work to be done are absolutely inefficient and wasteful. When relating to organizations, I mean incompetence in the broadest of terms.

In the marketplace, your company may be competing with a handful of competitors or countless competitors. Competence determines the grade of product or service you are providing to your customers and offering to potential customers. Your competitor may offer a better version of your product, and hence from the customer's perspective, they are a more competent supplier of goods. By comparison, your ability to offer quality goods is an incompetent attempt because you are operating at a level below industry standards.

## PERSONAL SWOT ANALYSIS

Raising your overall level of competency begins with a critical appraisal of your strengths, weaknesses, opportunities, and threats (SWOT). Most people think of a SWOT Analysis in terms of an organizational strategic planning tool. However, a SWOT Analysis can also be useful as a personal appraisal tool if you use it honestly to answer the hard questions. When coaching or counseling people I often use this method to help them paint a realistic 3D picture of themselves and why people perceive them the way they do. Additionally, the SWOT Analysis helps to identify why a person views himself or herself the way he or she does. If the focus of an individual is first upon his or her weaknesses and threats, it can often lead to learning why he or she has a negative self-image.

Some years ago I was involved with counseling recovering drug and alcohol addicts as well as abused and homeless women and children. For these people, finding weaknesses and threats in their own lives was easy. Finding something positive to use as a foundation to build on was very, very difficult for many, if not most of these people. They just could not see anything good about themselves regardless of how many times they were encouraged. Sometimes the hard questions have nothing to do with your weaknesses or threats. Often we are our own worse critics, and finding our strengths and opportunities can present a difficult challenge. Over the years of speaking to groups large and small, I have found that all types of people struggle with the same challenge of pinpointing their strengths as those who struggle with addictions or other personal demons. Make no mistake; honest and critical self-evaluation is a difficult, but an absolutely indispensible tool in building and identifying competence and excellence.

Your strengths and weaknesses will deal directly with matters of the heart – who you really are inside and out and the habits you really have. Some strengths to consider may be found in your past experiences. Where have you been? What have you seen? What wisdom can you squeeze out of these experiences and apply to other areas of your life or situations and challenges you currently face? For example, my oldest daughter has been to over 30 of the 50 United States by the age of 13. She has been to every major city on the west coast, walked the streets of New York City, seen the monuments in Washington D.C., enjoyed the sun of Orlando, Florida, and experienced the multi-cultural city of Vancouver, British Columbia, Canada to name a few of her experiences. One of her greatest strengths is her ability to get along with people from all over the country and to see the value in many different types of people and types of cultures. Our family has intentionally made a point of exposing our daughters to many different places in our country. As a graduation present we are planning a family trip to see Europe and experience the rich history that serves as a foundation for our Western culture here in the United States.

Look intently for value in your experiences; even the small ones. There are other questions to be asked concerning your strengths. What are your educational experiences? What work experience (even volunteer work is work) or specific trade knowledge do you have? What are some of your strong personal traits, such as work ethic, self discipline, optimism, or creativity? Are you a social person who is comfortable speaking to individuals and groups?

All of these are examples of strengths you need to consider about yourself when contemplating your level of competence in relation to your stated pursuits.

When considering your weaknesses, it is important that the process is completed in the most mature manner possible. There can be no self-loathing or negative thinking about your self-worth. Your attitude should exude confidence in your strengths while taking a hard and realistic look at areas that need improvement so they do not hinder future progress. For example, one of my weaknesses is food. I enjoy eating and spending community time with my friends and family. However, not just any food will do. I enjoy Italian food the most. The problem with this is my body type (meso-endomorphic) does not allow me to eat the copious amounts of Italian food that I would like. In fact, I often joke that my metabolism is so slow, if it sped up it might stop! I can walk past a table full of deserts and gain five pounds without eating a bit of it! It is terrible! While I may be exaggerating a little, I am sure you get the point. If left unattended, my weight *could* spiral out of control and cause serious health problems for me down the road. Lying in a hospital makes it difficult to achieve my goals and the reality of a weight problem due to poor habits is something I have to be aware of before it becomes a serious threat. Often our weaknesses can give entrance to our threats, and this is the case for my weakness to overeat.

There are questions you need to ask yourself when considering your weaknesses. Do I lack the experience or education to exhibit competence in my chosen pursuits? If so, what skills or knowledge do I lack? What personal habits (such as overeating) that could cause potentially serious threats to my well being and pursuits do I need to overcome in order to achieve my goals? Do I have the type of personality that attracts people to me or repels people away from me? Do the people I spend the most time with while not at work lift me up and influence me in a positive way? Do they speak negatively about my dreams and about me personally? Are they indifferent, and thus do they influence me to be indifferent about my pursuits? All of these are examples of questions you need to ask when critically examining your weaknesses.

Opportunities and threats deal directly with how well you see external opportunities and threats that relate to your chosen pursuits in life. If you cannot see the opportunities around, you there is no hope that you will ever be able to capture them and capitalize on conditions or resources that are available. For millennia humankind lived much the same way. Few substantial advances in technology were made for almost 3,000 years until men and women began to observe things that were always present but from a different perspective. For instance, humankind had not observed steam as a productive resource until one day in 1698, Thomas Savery was attempting to pump water out of a coalmine and utilized steam to force water upwards and out of the mine shaft. This first step helped him to invent the first crude steam engine. Then shortly thereafter, another inventor named Thomas Newcomen improved on Savery's invention by introducing steam into a cylinder producing a more sophisticated version of the first engine. Less than a generation later, James Watt made improvements on the Newcomen cylinder that led to the steam machines used to power the industrial revolution. These advancements led to the combustible engine, which ultimately led to every new advancement humankind has made in engine driven transportation.

The first century Roman philosopher Lucius Annaeus Seneca (also known as Seneca the Younger, 4 BCE-65 CE) once observed, "Luck is what happens when preparation meets opportunity." The first step to capturing our opportunities is to prepare our minds to see them when they arrive. Here are some questions to help you see current or future opportunities. Is there a need for my skills or my company's product or service regionally, nationally, or globally? What new certifications or degrees are currently being offered that would enhance my career? What unique opportunities or personal acquaintances does my current career afford to me, and how can I utilize those to achieve my pursuits? What industries do not use people who have my skill sets but would be impacted greatly if they did utilize them (for example, utilizing Six Sigma in a field other than manufacturing)? Am I selling what potential clients or employers are buying, or am I trying to sell others on what I am selling regardless of what they are buying? The difference is subtle, but no less profound. You have to sell clients what they are buying. If they are buying apples, sell them apples. Questions like these help to open your mind to opportunities that are present yet rarely recognized.

Unseen or unaccounted threats will derail the best-laid plans. Risk management on a personal level means taking a look around at the conditions and environments that could cause you to fall short of your goals or hinder the progress you would like to make in a worthwhile pursuit. When I was in the United States Navy, I used to deliver a brief (entitled, ORM – Operational Risk Management) to the sailors in my squadron concerning recreational hazards during the summer and winter months. Identifying threats allowed the sailors to prepare for conditions that could sneak up on them if they were trapped or otherwise stuck hiking, fishing, or skiing in the wilderness. Every year people died out on the mountains near our base, and almost every time the reason was lack of preparation due to not properly assessing the threats to safety and health. Each day people's careers and personal lives are shattered because they failed to properly prepare for the journey toward their stated pursuits. The failure to assess possible threats leaves them vulnerable to conditions and situations to arise and derail their dreams.

Often people go beyond failing to account for risks and actually ignore them as if they are bullet-proof or invincible. A story told by Gaius Suetonius Tranquillus (69/70 CE-after 130 CE), in his work *Lives of the Twelve Caesars (Caesar 80-82)*, tells of the circumstances surrounding the death (on March 15, 44 BCE) of the most famous Caesar of them all – Julius Caesar. The text is a bit lengthy, but I believe worth inclusion due to its clear illustration concerning the danger of not preparing for threats or ignoring them altogether.

> "In order to avoid giving assent to this proposal the conspirators hastened the execution of their designs. Therefore the plots which had previously been formed separately, often by groups of two or three, were united in a general conspiracy, since even the populace no longer were pleased with present conditions, but both secretly and openly rebelled at his tyranny and cried out for defenders of their liberty. On the admission of foreigners to the Senate, a placard was posted: 'God bless the commonwealth! Let no one consent to point

out the House to a newly made Senator.' The following verses too were repeated everywhere:

The Gauls he dragged in triumph through the town
Caesar has brought into the Senate house
And changed their breeches for the purple gown.

When Quintus Maximus, whom he had appointed consul in his place for three months, was entering the theater, and his lictor in the usual manner called attention to his arrival, a general shout was raised: 'He's no Consul!' After the removal of Caesetius and Marullus from office as tribunes, they were bound to have not a few votes at the next elections of consuls. Some wrote on the base of Lucius Brutus' statue, 'Oh, that you were still alive'; and on that of Caesar himself:

Because he drove from Rome the royal race,
Brutus was first made consul in their place.
This man, because he put the consuls down,
has been rewarded with a royal crown.

More than sixty joined the conspiracy against him, led by Gaius Cassius and Decimus and Marcus Junius Brutus. At first they hesitated whether to form two divisions at the elections in the Field of Mars, so that while some hurled him from the bridge as he summoned the tribes to vote, the rest might wait below and slay him; or to set upon him in the Sacred Way or at the entrance to the theater. When, however, a meeting of the Senate was called for the ides of March in the Hall of Pompey, they readily gave that time and place the preference.

Now Caesar's approaching murder was foretold to him by unmistakable signs. A few months before, when the settlers assigned to the colony at Capua by the Julian Law were demolishing some tombs of great antiquity, to build country houses, and plied their work with the greater vigor because as they rummaged about they found a quantity of vases of ancient workmanship, there was discovered in a tomb, which was said to be that of Capys, the founder of Capua, a bronze tablet, inscribed with Greek words and characters to this effect: 'Whenever the bones of Capys shall be discovered, it will come to pass that a descendant of his shall be slain at the hands of his kindred, and presently avenged at heavy cost to Italy.' And let no one think this tale a myth or a lie, for it is vouched for by Cornelius Balbus, an intimate friend of Caesar.

Shortly before his death, as he was told, the herds of horses which he had dedicated to the river Rubico when he crossed it, and had let loose without a keeper, stubbornly refused to graze and wept copiously. Again, when he was offering sacrifice, the soothsayer Spurinna warned him to beware of danger, which would come not later than the ides of March. On the day before the ides of that month a little bird called the king-bird flew into the Hall of Pompey with a sprig of laurel, pursued by others of various kinds from the grove hard by, which tore it to pieces in the hall. In fact the very night before his murder he dreamt now that he was flying above the clouds, and now that he was clasping the hand of Jupiter; and his wife Calpurnia thought that the pediment of their house fell, and that her husband was stabbed in her arms; and on a sudden the door of the room flew open of its own accord.

Both for these reasons and because of poor health he hesitated for a long time whether to stay at home and put off what he had planned to do in the Senate. But at last, urged by Decimus Brutus not to disappoint the full meeting, which had for some time been waiting for him, he went forth almost at the end of the fifth hour. When a note revealing the plot was handed him by someone on the way, he put it with others which he held in his left hand, intending to read them presently. Then, after many victims had been slain, and he could not get favorable omens, he entered the House in defiance of portents, laughing at Spurinna and calling him a false prophet, because the ides of March were come without bringing him harm. Spurinna replied that they had of a truth come, but they had not gone.

As he took his seat, the conspirators gathered about him as if to pay their respects, and straightway Tillius Cimber, who had assumed the lead, came nearer as though to ask something. When Caesar with a gesture put him off to another time, Cimber caught his toga by both shoulders. As Caesar cried, 'Why, this is violence!', one of the Cascas stabbed him from one side just below the throat. Caesar caught Casca's arm and ran it through with his stylus, but as he tried to leap to his feet, he was stopped by another wound. When he saw that he was beset on every side by drawn daggers, he muffled his head in his robe, and at the same time drew down its lap to his feet with his left hand, in order to fall more decently, with the lower part of his body also covered. And in this wise he was stabbed with three and twenty wounds, uttering not a word, but merely a groan at the first stroke, though some have written that when Marcus Brutus rushed at him, he said in Greek, 'You too, my child?'

All the conspirators made off, and he lay there lifeless for some time, until finally three common slaves put him on a litter and carried him home, with one arm hanging down. And of so many wounds none, in the opinion of the physician Antistius, would have proved mortal except the second one in the breast."

*translated by Joseph Gavorse*

Julius Caesar created the conditions through which real threats ultimately took his life by ignoring his weaknesses and then ignoring threats he knew were probably present. Ignoring threats do not make them go away. People who believe that if you ignore something long enough it will magically go away are only fooling themselves. Ignoring problems only multiplies them. Here are a few questions you need to ask when considering future threats. What is the long-term outlook for people with my skill set? Am I in a field or possess a skill set that is growing obsolete? What is the attitude in the private and government sectors concerning my pursuits? Is becoming an elite provider of my services or goods possible, or are there new technologies or practices that are taking its place? What sort of economic cycle will kill any pursuit of my dreams? I ran into this problem when the economy collapsed in late 2008 and 2009. An investor and I had formed an automobile company with an untraditional sales model just in time for the auto industry to fall apart. We failed to read the economic mile markers, and it cost us our entire investment. This was definitely a lesson learned for both of us. These are all good examples of the types of questions you need to ask when assessing your threats.

After completing the SWOT portion of the exercise, it is now time to analyze the data and see exactly how these bits of information support or prohibit your pursuits. In my experience, the more strengths a person has and the more opportunities a person is aware of, often indicates a higher level of competence than those facing serious weaknesses and threats. I cannot stress enough that the subject of competency lays bare every person equally and sets them on a level playing field. A look at the competency of an individual strips them of academic achievement, political power, positional authority, or achievements and asks the question, "Despite your level of education and professional experience, what have you accomplished in relation to your stated pursuits, and how completely do you fulfill your responsibilities and obligations?" The mailroom carrier who forgets to deliver mail to the proper people is just as incompetent as the CEO who squanders millions of dollars. Admittedly, the incompetence of both examples is of different scope and has different consequences but both suffer the same condition: incompetence to perform the role they were hired to play. Incompetence is a condition that often becomes terminal. Comedian Ron White famously said, *"You can't fix stupid."* I say, you cannot fix incompetent, either. There are not doctors for the stupid and incompetent because the patient can only cure these ills. The cure for stupid is education and better choices. The cure for incompetence is education and action that produces intended results. In both instances, the infected have to want to be cured.

# THE FOUR STAGES OF COMPETENCE
# – PERSONAL

During the 1940s, renowned psychologist Abraham Maslow (who gave us the famous Hierarchy of Needs in 1943) developed the conscious competence theory, more popularly known in academic circles as the Four Stages of Learning (or the Four Stages of Competence). The conscious competence theory describes how people range in competence from unconscious *in*competence to unconscious competence and how they move through the different levels of competence through learning (academic or experiential). Through the years numerous leadership and teaching gurus have come and gone, and many tried to put their own spin on Maslow's conscious competence theory, passing Maslow's originality off as their own. These gurus should be of dubious reputation. After almost 20 years of reading and leading I have found there are very few "new" ideas, especially in regard to subjects as well covered as leadership or learning. The reason I am referencing Maslow so heavily in this chapter is because I want you to know where the idea came from originally so you can do your own research about the subject later. Maslow's contributions to learning and psychology are probably some of the most important progressions made in the subject during the 20$^{th}$ century. What we are doing here is taking the conscious competence theory and giving it a different application so we can see magnified results in our personal and organizational competences.

## *The Four Stages of Learning and their explanation are:*

1. **Level 1 - Unconscious Incompetence:** Unconscious Incompetence is the state when a person lacks the knowledge of how to accomplish a task, is unaware that he or she should even need to know how to accomplish the task in the first place, and thus has no desire to learn how to accomplish a certain task. Most introductory training should begin at this level when dealing with new subject matter or new personnel being exposed to industry information for the first time. An example of this is when a senior manager is exposed to TQM or Six Sigma and how it applies

to and can ultimately benefit his company. Often the initial response is resistance because he or she does not know what he or she does not know, does not know the possible benefits, and therefore does not have a reason to care.

2. **Level 2 - Conscious Incompetence:** Conscious Incompetence is the state when a person is aware that he or she does not have the understanding or the skills required to complete a task and he or she is aware of *the need* to gain these understandings and skill sets. A good example of this is when a college student is introduced to an area of study that intrigues him enough to pursue the subject but at this point he lacks the understanding and skills of the discipline to be of any helpful use professionally.

3. **Level 3 - Conscious Competence:** Conscious Competence is the state most people operate in on a daily basis in relation to their trained vocation. In this state, a person is aware of the principles and finer points of a task or skill set and, through concentrated effort, executes the task or skill flawlessly. A good example of this would be a project manager who is involved in managing a project that has multiple deliverables, budgets, and deadlines and meets all of these requirements through focused effort and attention. If the project manager were to take his eye off of the ball, he could cause huge problems for his project. This is why the project manager focuses on what has to be done and employs his understanding and project management skill sets to achieving each task.

4. **Level 4 - Unconscious Competence:** Unconscious Competence is also known as "second nature" or someone being "a natural" at a certain skill set. At this level of competence, the person instinctively responds to situations and environments without having to think

through the proper steps. An example of this is when a military member or member of the police or fire department is faced with a dire situation that requires reflexive action and the person responds exactly as he has trained himself to respond. No thinking through steps or focused attention to specific processes is required. Achieving this level of competence requires years of experience and training. Understanding alone cannot propel an individual to this level; both experience *and* understanding are required to achieve the level.

Personal competence that is useful in a productive environment exists at the Conscious Competence level (Level 3) and over time *may* eventually progress to the Unconscious Competence level (Level 4). Progression through these levels is *not* a foregone conclusion and nothing guarantees that anyone has the potential to be competent in any given skill set. For example, I am an absolutely terrible basketball player. In fact, the last time I played basketball was almost 10 years ago, and I broke my ankle in the process. No amount of training or practice is going to move me from Level 2 to Level 3. Even if I wanted to make the leap mentally (which I do not), I just do not have the potential physically. There is this silly notion floating around leadership blogs and performance consultants (so they can sell more products) that everyone has the potential to be an effective leader or an elite manager. Nothing could be farther from the truth. Everyone *does not* have the potential to be a leader, trainer, manager, or guru in the same way that everyone does not have the potential to be a star wide receiver in the National Football League or a Sumo Wrestler in Japan. There are physical and mental limitations that stunt our potential for some things. I cannot tell you how many people I have coached or counseled over the years who have had a negative self image or felt as if they were forever trapped under a cloud of condemnation because they were not "good enough" to reach their potential when the reality all along was the person never had the potential to be a leadership superstar or manager extraordinaire in the first place. People who are content with not leading or managing still have a huge potential to influence your organization for the better but in a different role. There is much to be said for the person who is loyal, thoughtful, accurate, kind, and consistent with his or her work. If you could hire an army of these types of people, your productivity issues would virtually disappear.

Like any skill set, leadership and management can be learned, but this fact alone does not mean everyone has the interest or the ability to learn the skills necessary to lead and manage and then apply them effectively. A better way to frame the statement would be to say that leadership is a teachable subject. Leadership and management *can be* learned, but that does not mean leadership and management *will be* learned by anyone who studies it. When I was in the Navy, we had guys who came up through the ranks but never showed any potential for leadership or management at the organizational level. Most of these people were wonderful technicians and could solve just about any technical problem, but when it came to leading others or managing projects or programs they would often times fail or produce mediocre results. These sailors were great support people and became the strong go-to technicians on the team but were not people you would want to run your shop for an extended period because they never showed an interest in learning and grasping the finer points of leadership and management. In our shop, that was fine. We knew the extent of each one of our sailor's ability to lead and manage. Occasionally, we would put these people into positions to grow by stretching their leadership or management comfort zone, but never on a consistent basis. We always tried to keep people in their productive elements and let them contribute in areas that they displayed Conscious Competence (Level 3) or Unconscious Competence (Level 4).

You need to determine these same levels within your organization. When it comes to leadership and management, at which level (Level 1 to Level 4) is each of your people? Is your Human Resources Coordinator a Level 1 on leadership but a Level 4 on Employment Law? Utilize his or her talent and interest for Employment Law, but do not try to square the circle by forcing him or her to try to learn skills he or she has no tendency or interest to learn. This will breed self-condemnation, frustration, and discontent in an otherwise outstanding employee.

# HOW TO MENTOR THROUGH THE FOUR LEVELS OF COMPETENCY

Before we get into the process of mentoring people through the Four Levels of Competency, we need to address a few fundamental ideas about training in general. Consider these to be prerequisites for the larger mentoring process:

1.  **Start at the Right Level:** Proper assessment of competency level is the key to starting an individual at the proper level of learning. Often Human Resource departments and training companies assume people are at the Conscious Incompetence level (Level 2 - they know that they do not know) and begin the mentoring process too high. Often, people are still at the Unconscious Incompetence level (Level 1 – they do not know what they do not know) and are completely lost in relation to the material being reviewed. Several years ago, I was sitting in a class where Life, Health, and Disability Insurance were being taught for a licensing exam. The course material assumed the students had certain knowledge and fundamental understanding of the insurance industry and a bit about finance as well. I had a keen interest in the subject and pretty solid investment and business management experience, so I managed to work my way through the material easily; however, several of my fellow students had a very difficult time understanding how concepts and products worked fundamentally because they had never been exposed to the basic ideas at the root of the concepts being taught. These people lacked an introduction to the material formulated with a Level 1 learner in mind. Subsequently, several of them failed the exam.

2.  **Make Sure you Teach the *Why's* Before the *What's* and *How's*:** If all you know is facts and figures and you never learn the *why's* and *how's* associated with them, you will never be able to apply the knowledge in a profitable manner. I find this is the case with most training programs available today. The programs have

119

wonderful information that is well presented and easy to understand, but the student comes away with a lot of *what* knowledge and little if any *why* and *how* knowledge. This is the reason so many people go to the conferences and seminars and come away fired up with a bunch of knowledge that three months later has not profited them a bit. What is the use of gaining knowledge if you have no understanding of *why* and *how* to apply it? Often, a lack of application is due to fear of failure, and fear of failure is usually the result of a lack of confidence in knowing *why* the subject matter works and *how* it works.

3. **Employ Ockham's Razor:** This may seem elementary, but it is often overlooked. If you try to teach a complicated subject in a complicated manner, even the most able minded people will be lost. Any machine or method with a large amount of moving parts has a greater risk of failure than a machine or method that has a few moving parts. The idea of using simplicity for explaining an argument or a philosophical position is often known as Ockham's Razor, named after the 14th-century theologian and logician named William Ockham (1285-1349) who often employed the strategy in his writings. During my training sessions, I call the simplification of concepts and processes the "Barney Style" approach, so-named after the famous purple dinosaur who entertained children on television for a number of years. When deciding on different teaching methods, remember to use Ockham's razor and to "Barney Style" the information.

4. **Practice Patience:** I learned this prerequisite through being a parent to two beautiful and often complicated girls. My girls have physical attributes and personalities that could not be more different. One is tall. The other is short. One has brown hair. The other has naturally blonde highlights. One is dark skinned. The other has

a fair complexion. One has hazel green eyes. The other, dark brown. As for their personalities, one is quiet, and the other is loud. One is very stoic and logical. The other is very emotional and sensitive. One holds grudges. The other lets things go. One is guarded. The other is touchy feely. One understands conceptually. The other learns hands-on. Both are absolutely amazing girls who bring home straight A's, play sports, and are involved in civic philanthropy. When parenting and coaching these girls, I have to be patient to communicate information to them in a way they can understand. Just as is the case with my two girls, no two people in your company will be the same. You will need to employ patience when communicating ideas and principles to people who find themselves on the Unconscious Incompetence level (Level 1) and the Conscious Incompetence level (Level 2). Often you will receive blank stares after masterfully explaining concepts to no avail. Here's a tip: Just because you think you delivered a great teaching, does not mean your message was received or understood by the audience. The true measure of speech mastery is not found in how the message was delivered but in how the message was received. Learning how to communicate effectively requires the employment of patience. If you stay committed to sharing truths with your employees and help them to grow personally and professionally, your patience will pay huge dividends later.

Utilizing these four prerequisites will propel your company's training program far above others who fail to employ them. If the person you are seeking to train is you, each of these foundational principles are still required. It is important for you to properly assess your own competency level (be honest about this), understand the fundamentals, keep things simple, and be patient with yourself as you move through the levels. There is no standard time frame to move from one level to another. Each person moves through the levels at their own pace according to their own potentials. Now, let us discuss how to mentor others through the four levels of learning.

## *Level 1 - Unconscious Incompetence:*

Unconscious Incompetence occurs in everyone's life to some degree or another. Being unaware and unable is a land we all must pass through on our journey toward personal and professional competency. Unfortunately, some people never finish the journey and decide to take up permanent residency there. Unconscious Incompetence is one of those unavoidable realities that when embraced becomes a great source of childlike wonder and when denied often becomes the pathway to personal and professional delusion. *You will never know what you do not know and you will never do what you have never done unless something or someone exposes you to information or methodology that illuminates a new set of possibilities.* This is why collaboration is so important. Without this exposure there is no hope for growth. When this exposure happens, we are given a choice to follow the pathway to competence or to settle in the land of Unconscious Incompetence having denied that we ever heard so much as a rumor about anything different than what we already know. In that moment, we have chosen denial as our path and defined the rest of our journey. This becomes our defining moment.

I remember one of my defining moments. I was thirteen years old at the time. During my childhood, I moved quite a bit. I like to say my family was geographically schizophrenic. By the time I graduated from high school, I had been to nine different schools in almost as many different places. During that stage of my life, I was a very depressed and insecure young man. My grades were terrible, girls were not interested in me, I was overweight, I was a loner at school, and I even tried committing suicide but was too scared to follow through. One evening my father told me we would be leaving Oregon (where things were bad) and moving back to my home state of California. I was elated at the idea of this geographical fix. After the move, the world seemed a bit brighter and the grass a bit greener. I could almost see what looked like hope on the horizon. Unfortunately, the bliss would be short lived. Six weeks after we moved back to California, my father came to me and told me that he disliked his job and that we were moving back to Oregon. This was the beginning of my defining moment. I remember walking back to my room, shutting my door, sitting on a box I had not yet unpacked, and starting to cry. In that moment, I realized I was tired of being depressed and sad all of the time. I was tired of my happiness being at the mercy of everyone else's decisions. In that moment, I decided I was going to be myself and do what it took to make myself happy. As a young man, I accepted the idea that if my life was going to be what I dreamed it should be – it was up to me to make it happen. After I returned to Oregon, I was a different young man. My grades improved dramatically. I lost a huge amount of weight and started bodybuilding and playing sports again. In that moment on that box in Manteca, California, I had a defining event that would be the first of many I have had in my life.

As you read about my defining moment, begin to think about defining moments in your own life. If you cannot recall any defining moments from your past, realize that you are having one right now. Right now, you have a choice to deny truths and opportunities that you face, or you can accept the places where "the baby is ugly" and begin to learn strategies for growing in those areas. If you choose them to be, any moment can be a defining moment.

Some may call this defining moment an *"ah-ha moment."* An *"ah-ha moment"* occurs when the fog clears, the lights come on, and all of the sudden you become aware (or conscious) of the need to build new skill sets or learn new information. Sometimes this moment can help you discover the purpose in which you want to invest your life. When these moments occur, you realize that you have options you never knew existed, and the options have actions attached to them that you never knew you could do. Another world opens to you, and suddenly you feel alive. Level 1 can be considered a blissful slumber in which you are unaware of the potentials and possibilities surrounding you. Then something wakes you up – *a catalyst*. A catalyst can be anything that triggers you out of unconsciousness and into consciousness. A catalyst turns the lights on. I enjoy acting as a catalyst to wake people from their unconsciousness. Sometimes people do not like to be woken up. Sometimes people would rather sleep than become aware of incompetency or areas of growth opportunity. There is no way to help these people until they decide they want to help themselves or be helped. If you find yourself in a position to be a catalyst in someone's life or in the growth of an organization, make sure to capitalize on those opportunities when they arise because when they pass, often they do not travel that way again. If you happen to see someone or an organization that is acting as a catalyst in *your life* to move you from Level 1 to Level 2, it is wise to listen because when they pass, often they do not travel that way again (sound familiar?). *The key to moving from Level 1 to Level 2 is embracing an "ah-ha moment" and using it as a catalyst.*

## Level 2 - Conscious Incompetence:

Becoming aware of blind spots can create several different responses from people. Some people welcome the experience of learning about situations and information of which they were not previously aware. Some people bristle and climb into an insecure defensive posture and spout excuses until you leave them alone. In fact, it has been my observation from years of dealing with people who have had to come to the realization that they are incompetent in certain areas that their responses often follow a less intense version of the grieving process. Often the initial reaction is denial. Denial turns into anger and shifting responsibility through blaming other people or outside influences. Anger then gives way to sadness and depression. This usually brings a feeling uselessness, insufficiency, and self-loathing. From depression comes a time of bargaining in an attempt to secure the same desired outcome without the personal or professional investment and commitment required to overcome incompetence. From bargaining comes acceptance of the deficiencies that cause incompetence in certain areas. Once you are conscious of your incompetence and accept the condition as a reality, the opportunity for growth is wide and reaching.

Often people become overwhelmed by the realization of how much they do not know. The more you know, the more you realize how much you do not know. In this way, we are all stuck in some way in Conscious Incompetence, even as we move forward and answer questions and grow in knowledge and skills. The fact that a master manager and leader like Peter Drucker managed and led at the Unconscious Competence level (Level 4) does not mean that he did not have areas of new discovery that resided in Conscious Incompetence. The Four Stages of Learning is not a zero sum exercise where it is all or nothing. Often leadership materials present leadership and management in this fashion, and this idea is absolutely false. Everybody employs leadership at some point in their lives, and the exercise of this leadership is to varying degrees and applications. Few things are as pretentious and annoying as someone who believes that because he or she holds a position of leadership in one application he or she holds an influence of leadership in all situations. This also applies to competence as well. A close second in pretension is the person who believes competency in one area translates to competency in all areas. Life is not one dimensional in that way. The earlier you realize this reality, the farther and faster down the road to competency you will find yourself.

Once you have accepted the idea that you are incompetent in certain areas, you need to determine if this is an area where you have the potential to grow to the Conscious Competence level or not. Let me give you an example from my life in an area of complete incompetence. I am terrible at product sales. I am just not good at it. On a scale of one to ten, with one being the lowest and ten being the highest, I would rate about a negative three. I have read book after book and been to seminar after seminar, and I just never got the hang of it. I am conscious of the fact that I am incompetent at product sales. After trying time and again to understand and apply the concepts of selling products, I always fail on the application side because I simply do not like doing what it takes to sell products. All of the phone calls and emails and letters cause me to freak out. I am a black and white kind of guy. Either you want the damn product or you don't. The product does this and that, and it provides the solution for this need and that one too. It will cost you $1,500, and no, I will not discount the price because I priced it right to begin with so that you will get the best value and so that I will make a profit. So, do you want the damn widget or not? That is my perspective on product sales, which is probably why I am a terrible salesman. I am not good at fluffing things for the sake of separating people from their money. I tried to learn how to fluff things, and it made me feel dishonest. This feeling of dishonesty made me feel uncomfortable at a very deep level morally and intellectually, and this created an internal conflict with my moral compass, which is why I am not able to move forward to a level of Conscious Competence in selling products.

Raising capital for a venture or presenting plans and projects to executives and CEO's is a different subject altogether, even though one could reasonably say that these actions are selling. I can raise capital. When I was 22 years old, I raised a very large sum of money in cash and available credit to start my first business (which was a magnificent failure and a wonderful learning experience). In the past, I have successfully presented large plans and projects to key players from the CEO level down. For several years, I travelled and spoke to large and small groups about leadership and management and sold these audiences on the ideas I was presenting and the material I had to offer. The reason I was successful in these endeavors is because I believed in what I was communicating. When I was learning how to present ideas in an effective manner, I believed in the need to learn these techniques, and I absolutely believed in the technique itself. Both were required to find success. When you have a deep belief that what you need to learn and the application of what you have learned are within the scope of your potential to execute them, nothing can stop you from moving to a Conscious Competence level.

Fifteen years ago, I did not wake up and say I was going to go sell people on the principles of leadership and then find immediate success. Fifteen years ago, I read my first self-help book, *How to Win Friends and Influence People* by Dale Carnegie, and then I found everything I could read about the subject of communication, leadership, and management. Shortly after I read Mr. Carnegie's seminal work, I joined Toastmaster's International and worked my way up through the different levels of competency. I competed every three months in speaking competitions and analyzed why I won and why I lost competitions. I joined the local Chamber of Commerce and interacted with local small business leaders and asked questions about their companies and what they felt made them successful and what caused them the most challenge. I listened to their stories and their experiences, and I took copious notes. Almost every night I would stand by myself in front of a full-length mirror, and I would look myself eye to eye and deliver my speeches (I still do this), trying new ways of speaking or new mannerisms to accentuate the message and smooth the presentation. When riding alone in my car, I would talk and sing and make all sorts of strange noises with my voice as loud as I could possibly stand (which made for some interesting looks and finger pointing from fellow drivers) so that I would be absolutely comfortable with the sound of my own voice (I learned this technique from Gerry Spence's book entitled *How to Argue and Win Every Time*). I was fully engaged in training myself to do what it was going to take to be successful and to be competent in speaking and teaching.

The only way to move from Level 2 to Level 3 is through training yourself to learn skill sets that fall within areas of potentiality. Coaches and trainers call this training your strengths. An example of this would be an offensive lineman who plays football and engages in heavy weightlifting for power, a bit of cardiovascular exercise for stamina, and agility training for footwork. The offensive lineman will not be catching 200 footballs every practice. He will not be training his footwork to catch footballs on the sideline. He will not be running sprints and running routes to shake defensive backs. Why? He does not have the potential to become competent as a wide receiver. Instead, he focuses on his potential and the skills required for being a top quality offensive lineman. You must begin to engage in regularly scheduled training in areas of your greatest potential to build your core competences in areas of incompetence. *The key to moving from Level 2 to Level 3 is training in areas of your greatest potential.*

## Level 3 - Conscious Competence:

This is the level where 95% of executives and business people plateau and find comfortable satisfaction. To be clear, there is nothing wrong with settling at this level of competence. At this level, business is completed, and it is done right. The only training that is involved at this level is refining skills and eliminating waste from daily routines and business practices. Usually people in this level of competency serve as catalysts for those in Level 1 and trainers for those in Level 2. *The key to moving from Level 3 to Level 4 is time, an authentic lifestyle, and a commitment to keep training your strengths.*

## Level 4 - Unconscious Competence:

What are you, really? You may do the work of an executive manager, but is an executive manager who you are on the inside? Why would anyone want to follow your leadership? If I were to answer those questions, I would say, "I fix things." Clients and friends know me as "the fixer." Everything I do or create is a result of the expression of this element of my personality and intellect. I think in terms of possibilities, solutions, and results, and I act in a manner consistent with my thinking. People and companies follow my leadership and advice because they know that I can get things done and that I will always take the time to help them achieve their individual goals because in doing so I help the company achieve its goals. It is important to note that not everybody finds my style of leadership something they can buy into and follow, and that is fine by me. There are plenty of leaders in this world who are better suited for these people to follow. My commitment to doing the right things right begins with me, and the people who do follow my lead know I will never hold them to a level of accountability that I have not held myself to first. Level 4 performance is only achievable by the undeniably authentic person. This is the level where you become a mentor and have enough natural instinct to dispense sage advice in almost every situation you or your company may face.

Think about this question for a moment: ***Why should anyone give you permission to lead him or her?*** Are you the type of leader who feels that people should follow you because of your position or title in a company? Did you attain your position due to nepotism? Were you given your position because of personal relationships or political favor? Unconscious Competence is not a result of whom you think you are, whom you desire to be, or who your parents are. As I mentioned earlier in the book, there is an old Irish proverb that expresses this idea succinctly: *"You have to do your own growin', no matter how tall your grandfather is."* This level of competence comes only to those who eat, sleep, live, and breathe their vocation. They make the position; the position does not make them.

One of my favorite movies is *Gladiator*, directed by Ridley Scott and starring Russell Crowe, Joaquin Phoenix, and Connie Neilson. In the opening scene, the Romans battle the German barbarians in what would be the last battle to win the war for the Romans. As the battle begins, Russell Crowe's character, General Maximus Decimus Meridius, rides side-by-side into battle with his men, unapologetic and unafraid. After the battle, General Maximus walks through his men checking on their condition and exchanging warm pleasantries. His character is genuinely interested in the well-being of his men. In return, his men have a deep loyalty to their General and afford him the highest respect soldiers can show toward one another – devotion unto death. Shortly after the battle is finished, Caesar Marcus Aurelius's son, Commodus, arrives at the camp acting like he is there to fight in the battle and asks his father, "Have I missed the battle?" His father replies, "You have missed the war." Yet even as Commodus missed the war, he still expected and required the same respect and devotion of the soldiers and officers as they have shown to General Maximus. This entire opening scene illustrates perfectly the difference between people who are genuinely at the Unconscious Competence level (Maximus) and those who feel entitled and have a lack the courage to do what it takes to achieve authentically this level of competency (Commodus).

The key for achieving Unconscious Competence can be found in a quote by Gandhi: "We must become the change we wish to see in the world." This level of competence comes when what you produce is merely the animation of what already resides inside of you. The reason dogs bark and birds chirp is because they are expressing the life – the competency – that resides inside of them. No thought is involved; they just bark or chirp because it is natural. Level 4 competences are not achieved by getting a degree or taking some classes. Level 4 competences are achieved through sheer dedication and ownership.

For example, if you were accused of murder, you could higher any number of run-of-the-mill defense lawyers who may or may not be able to get the charges against you dropped. Your other alternative is to hire a legendary attorney like Mr. Gerry Spence (assuming of course that he would take your case) who has never lost a criminal case neither as a prosecutor nor as a defense attorney. Additionally, he has not lost a civil case since 1969 and has had more multi-million dollar verdicts without an intervening loss than any lawyer in America - *ever*. Law and argument are expressions of who Gerry Spence is on the inside. Mr. Spence graduated from the University of Wyoming Law School in 1952 just like many other law school students. He is not an Ivy League alumnus with a pedigree of storied attorneys in his family tree. What separates Mr. Spence is that he internalized what he believed to be the pentacle of being an attorney by representing the poor, the injured, and the forgotten against big corporations and big government. What followed was a storied career unmatched in sincere dedication and undeniable results. Mr. Spence *is* an advocate, not merely a man who works in advocacy. Can others say the same about you? Can others look at you and say you *are* the work you perform? Is what you do an expression of the person inside? Why should anyone give you permission to lead them?

## LEVELS OF COMPETENCE – ORGANIZATIONAL

The fundamental ideas that undergird the four levels of competence on a personal level also undergird the levels of competence within organizations. We will not revisit the basic principles here but apply these principles in a new way to a larger environment.

The Four Stages of Learning and their explanation for organizations are:

1. **Level 1 - Unconscious Incompetence:** Unconscious Incompetence on an organizational level is the state when an organization lacks the knowledge of how to accomplish a business related process or task, is unaware that tools exist to accomplish certain processes or tasks (this is especially true with quality control and quality assurance related processes), or may not have a desire to learn how to properly apply these processes or tasks. In the marketplace, it is very important to stay up to date with the latest methodologies of quality management, process management, human resource management, and capital management. Companies that do not know what they do not know are in a dire competitive disadvantage to competitors who are aware of important business management information. Research and Development departments

make sure the organization is never lagging in innovation and always "in the know" in relation to product development. Human Resources and Executive Management generally are responsible to make sure their key players are always up to date with the latest training and management processes. "We didn't know" is never a right answer when asked why the competition has an advantage that your company could have seized earlier.

2. **Level 2 - Conscious Incompetence:** Conscious Incompetence on an organizational level is the state when an organization is aware that it does not have the understanding or the skill sets available to execute a process, project, or task to stay competitive. Additionally, senior management is generally aware of *the need* to gain these understandings and skill sets but often find themselves in a squabble over how to gain this required knowledge and these skill sets. If handled poorly, this could be a step where the company knows there is a problem but refuses to address the issue head-on and instead chooses to develop a work-around and justify the action by saying something to the affect of, "Sometimes you have to work with what you have" or "We are just playing cards we were dealt." Excuses like this are indicative of a larger and potentially more lethal problem with the management than knowing you are incompetent, which is *being content to stay that way*. Professional and personal courage must not allow excuses to take center stage when owning the situation and addressing it with focused attention is the order of the day. If an organization becomes accustomed to making excuses for inefficiency and failure, it will spread like cancer throughout the company and kill the organization.

3. **Level 3 - Conscious Competence:** Conscious Competence on an organizational level is the state where most profitable and well-managed organizations

operate on a daily basis. That is not to say that the company does not have areas where it can grow or progress in its competencies. What it does mean is that it provides the service or product for which it is in business to provide with competitive competency in relation to their primary competitors in the marketplace. In this state, the organization is aware of the principles and finer points of processes, projects, and skill-sets required to execute its business flawlessly. It has a beachhead in the market that becomes the unique selling proposition (or unique buying reason) that beats most, if not all, of their competitors. At Level 3, "good enough" is never good enough. Professionalism and excellence are the standard, and companies should hold every employee to these high standards. Purpose-driven execution (acts of intention) propels companies at the Conscious Competence level.

4. **Level 4 - Unconscious Competence:** Unconscious Competence on an organizational level is that thing the company naturally does or provides better than its competitor provides. Often the company does not have to work especially hard to produce these results. When providing your primary product or service with unparalleled excellence and professionalism becomes instinctive rather than resulting from conscious acts of intention, your company has achieved this level of competence. However, due to the constantly changing market conditions and the rate at which business methodologies and commerce move, it is very difficult to sustain this level of competence for long periods without unknowingly becoming complacent. Unconscious Competence, however, applies to more than your company's primary product or service. Some of the time Unconscious Competence applies to processes, products, or skill-sets that are not the primary product or service provided to the market. For example, I am currently doing work for an organization that provides a certain product in the

education industry. While this company does provide a quality primary product for its customers, the customers know the company best for the high level of customer service it provides. Its customer service attitude is a part of the atmosphere and culture it has created within the organization, and taking care of the customer better than the next competitor has become second nature. When problems arise, everyone from the front desk receptionist to the CEO instinctively knows to take care of the customer. There is no thinking about how to respond to the customer. They simply make the customer feel as if he or she is the most important customer the company has because *each* of its customers is the most important customer it has.

Achieving this level of competence as second nature in your company requires years of training and culture management by all hands in the organization. Understanding you must provide good customer service or quality products and services cannot propel an organization to this level; culture creation, experience, and intimate understanding are required to achieve it. This level is a direct result of the inherent culture of the company, and instinct takes over and triggers excellent responses.

## HOW TO LEAD YOUR ORGANIZATION THROUGH THE FOUR LEVELS OF COMPETENCY

Organizations are a singular composite of the many people who work for the organization. What we know as the personality of an individual is translatable to the culture of an organization. A person's personality drives his or her reaction to conditions within each of the levels of competence. In an organizational setting, the culture of the organization drives the reactions of the organization on a macro level. For example, if the company has a tendency to shoot first and ask questions later, the organization is probably full of people who are stuck in a crisis cycle leadership style. The company probably views everything as a crisis and like an addict gets high off the drama. Every organization is different culturally in the same way that every individual is different with respect to his or her personality and preferences. Before trying to make changes to a corporate culture, it is very important to determine the details of the corporate culture prior making recommendations and pitching a change initiative.

Flipping an organization on its head is an easy thing to do if you approach change, growth, or realignment from the wrong perspective. I have personally managed to mess this up and can tell you it is not fun to have to mend fences and re-launch a change initiative after everyone is upset or has lost confidence in your ability to lead. The truth is, more often than not, it is impossible to lead a successful initiative once you have offended or alienated the culture of an organization, especially if you are an outsider. It is my suggestion that you discern whether it would be better to walk softly and carry a big stick or walk softly and leave the stick at home. Some organizations need to feel the rod of correction, but you had better use wise judgment whether or not it is your role to wield it or not. If swinging the stick is not why they hired you or if you are not in a position to exercise the authority to swing the stick, leave it at home, even if the situation warrants someone getting a good thumping.

### *Level 1 - Unconscious Incompetence:*

Sometimes people and companies become so task focused that they forget to back away from the daily details of task completion to see the big picture. By big picture, I mean the *really* big picture that involves not only your company but the whole industry landscape in which your company lives. The reason your company does not know what it does not know is that it is not asking the right questions. The same principles used to coach individuals into self-discovery are the same principles organizations all over the world use to formulate discovery initiatives. If you want to have better information, you need to start asking better questions. Knowing what constitutes a better question requires education and training. Executives who do not know what questions to ask are of little use to the company that has aspirations of growing its market share and becoming a fixture in its industry. Often companies retain the services of consultants in these situations to supplement a shortfall of knowledge in this basic area. However, this only serves to bandage the immediate issue and does not address the larger root problem, which is that the executive did not have the professional knowledge to take the company where it needed to go. To be clear, I am not referring to complex and highly technical issues. I am referring to basic areas of business governance that competent management should be able to negotiate and overcome. If the leader driving the bus has no idea where he is going or that he is even supposed to be going anywhere in the first place, you have a grade-A problem on your hands. Remember, the company's problems (or your department's problems) are *your problems* whether you like it or not.

The most important part of asking the right questions is having the courage to listen to the answers. Often times you will hear information you do not want to hear. The art of asking questions is more than knowing what to ask. Knowing *how* to ask and *when* to ask are equally important to learning information about what your company is missing. Many (if not most) of the successful business people I know have a naturally curious constitution. In an organizational setting, this curiosity should drive your Research and Development (R&D) department. You may be thinking, "I run a small service business – why would I need Research and Development?" The answer to that is simple: There are always better, more efficient ways of deploying and delivering your service, even if it is a service as simple as cutting lawns or cleaning buildings. The bigger your service gets, the more you will need to research better delivery methods and develop a plan to deploy properly your service on a larger scale. No business is too simple for R&D.

Has your company thought about researching quality management, quality control, or quality assurance? The fact you are reading this book is proof you are already doing R&D and looking for better quality solutions for your business. Let me ask you about your accounting processes. Are you processing payables and receivables in the most efficient and professional manner appropriate for a business of your size? Has your company's growth outpaced your ability to keep up with its fiduciary responsibilities to itself? How can you maximize your sales and marketing efforts and synchronize both functions to work together seamlessly and produce more sales of higher quality customers? Do your methods and strategy support your company's stated purposes? If not, what would you need to do to realign your efforts to produce the intended result? Your company does not know what it does not know because it never bothers to ask. Most businesses muddle along with a *"good enough is good enough"* attitude and wonder why they cannot seem to break through the glass ceiling.

One of the first businesses I managed was a building services company. Before I led the company, I worked in the company stripping and waxing floors, cleaning toilets, dumping trash, cleaning windows, and working two days a week selling our services to prospective clients. Eventually, the owner saw that I had a talent for management and promoted me to General Manager. As the business grew from $150,000 in sales to $250,000 in sales a year, we hit a plateau that would not allow us to grow above $300,000 annually. After a full day of brainstorming that involved asking questions about every aspect of our services and our clients, the owner and I decided the reason for the plateau was due to the type of client we were targeting. We adjusted our approach and our customer profile and started to target a bigger customer. In short, the strategy worked, and we grew the business to almost $1 million in gross sales in about nine months. One session of determining what we were missing proved to be the catalyst for very profitable growth. When I left the business, it was the second largest non-franchise building services company in its region. That market position was a direct result of our practice of asking better questions. *The key to moving from Level 1 to Level 2 is backing away from the minutia and engaging in continuous and courageous research and development at all levels and every corner of the organization.*

## Level 2 - Conscious Incompetence:

Just because you have a product or service does not mean it is worth buying. Doing what you do better than the next person is not a new economic idea. Unfortunately, this idea *is* a new reality to the many business owners who start companies with an entitlement mentality. Just because you build your version of the widget does not mean the customers will come out to buy your widget versus your competitor's widget they are already buying. Even established companies often fall into the trap of believing that because they have been in their market for a long period or possibly have a controlling share of their market they are entitled to continued dominance. Here is the truth: ***There are no free lunches.*** There never has been, and there never will be a free lunch for marketplace leaders. Every day you have to get up and go get the business by being more competitive than the next person is.

Let me remind you of a lesson I pulled from nature. Each day a squirrel awakens early in morning, goes out amongst the trees, and finds his nut for the day. No one is going to bring a nut to this squirrel. The birds, the raccoons, the mice, and the insects all are on their own missions, driven by evolutionary and biological necessity to find their respective nuts for the day. The squirrel provides for his own sustenance and well-being. This analogy has the same moral as the early-bird-gets-the-worm lesson. A while back, my youngest daughter took a walnut shell, cleaned it up, and polished it. She gave it to me as a little gift to show her affection for me. What she did not know was the message it spoke to me about work ethic. I took that nut, put it in my office, and hung it on my wall (yes, that makes it a wall-nut). It reminds me every day that no matter how successful I become or what challenges I may face, like the squirrel, it is up to me to go out every day and get my nut. Every day I have to produce in order to keep my relationships and to provide a good lifestyle for my family. The process of production is going to be different for every type of business. Even companies in the same industry do business a little bit differently from the next person. However, all of them have to get up in the morning and go get their businesses' nut for the day.

If you have mentalities running through your company's culture that have created sacred cows, it is time to kill the cow and begin to continually evaluate and question everything at every step of your company's product or service creation and delivery system. However, you probably knew that. It is cliché to suggest a company go kill the sacred cow. So why have you not done it yet? Does fear prevent you? Are *you* the cow? Do you love the cow more than you desire to see real change in the conditions directly hampered by the presence of the cow? How would the improvement of your service or product quality affect your company and customers if you killed the cow?

Here are some more questions you need to be considering at this level of competence.

1. What is the voice of the customer saying they want?
2. How can you meet the needs of your customer base better than you currently do?
3. Is your current practice the most efficient and cost-effective method of executing internal processes?
4. Is your company as lean as it can be without being sick and anemic?
5. Are you effectively communicating to your customers why your company should be the only solution that can meet all of their needs?
6. How does your product or service *really* compare to the competition?

These are just a sampling of the questions you need to ask at this level in order to perfect your methods and products. Each of these questions can be summed up by asking, "Is this the best way, and if not, what is the best way?" Nevertheless, merely asking is not enough at this level. Execution is the order of the day. After asking the questions and the information has been gathered and organized into a cohesive plan of action, it is time to perfect the deficiencies through repetitive training and action. Perfecting the products or methods of your organization is not an academic exercise; it is a live-fire situation and will make or break your company's bid for profitability. When I was in the United States Navy, we constantly trained ourselves to execute our primary duties with excellence. If the execution of our training sessions was not done with excellence, we would retrain and execute the exercise again and again until we achieved the desired outcome. Sportsmen at all levels of competence practice their skills because ultimately they will perform in the game the way they practice, and so will your company. ***The key to moving from Level 2 to Level 3 is to keep asking questions and perfect your methods and products through continuous training.***

### *Level 3 - Conscious Competence:*

Often companies drift away from their niche in their markets by trying to please every customer all of the time and ultimately become useful to no one. The condition that drives this approach to business is insecurity and a lack of understanding what purpose and role the organization is supposed to play in the larger context of its market. Quite simply, companies often lose sight of whom they are and what market need they are supposed to fill. When your business is consciously competent, it focuses its efforts on what it does well, and its either trains to meet deficiencies or outsources those functions to other people or organizations that specialize in meeting those needs. There is no rule written anywhere that says your business has to be competent in everything all of the time. To stay relevant and profitable, your business must stay competent in those functions that distinguish it from the rest of the competition. In today's fiercely competitive market the odds that your business has many competitors is probably high. Staying close to your core values and doing certain things better than your competitors is what will carve out a niche in the marketplace and place you on defensible territory.

Very early in my career I was told time and again by very successful and wealthy older men to focus on one or two things that I was really good at and that I really enjoyed doing and to become so good at them that others would pay me to provide them as a service. During the early years of my adulthood, I searched for things I liked to do and things for which I showed a natural affinity. I tried several different things over the years, and in almost all of them, I fell short in some area. Either I enjoyed doing a certain task but just could not do it well enough to merit being paid very well (if at all) for providing it as a service, or I showed great promise and natural abilities but did not find enjoyment out of providing it as a service to others. Then in my mid-twenties, I began to work with the homeless, the addicted, the abused, and the distressed. Counseling with these people was challenging, and I found great satisfaction and good success. During these years, I found how much I truly loved teaching people how to win in life and how to overcome obstacles that stood in their pathways and prevented them from moving forward. I also began to work with non-profits and small business owners giving them advice and completing projects for their organizations. During my time of military service, I learned about risk management and quality assurance and found that many of the same principles I would use in working with people in pain and small business owners were the very same principles we employed to keep planes operational and to keep a 100% safety record. After my military service, I incorporated many of these principles into my work ethic, and my personal rate of success and feeling of satisfaction skyrocketed. Many of the principles in this book are a result of my focused efforts of shedding the things I was not competent in and zeroing in on those things I could provide at a very high level.

The same principles are true with your business. At this level, you must be very conscious of your core values and intentionally place these values at the heart of your business strategy. What drives your business? What sits at the center of everything you do on a daily basis in your workshops? Why do you build the products you build or provide the services you provide? Answering these types of questions will help you to identify what your core values are and shape the strategy required to achieve your purposes. *The key to moving from Level 3 to Level 4 is being true to your core values and allowing them to drive your strategy.*

## Level 4 - Unconscious Competence:

The well-known company GE does not have to think about how to build home appliances. It has been in *the* home appliance business for a very long time, and there probably are not very many things it does not know about how to engineer, build, and sell appliance products. Similarly, the Ford Motor Company does not have to think about how to build a good truck. It has had the number one selling truck for well over 25 years and has been in the auto business for the better part of a century. Instinct is an intangible tool that wields a powerful benefit to the organization that has become so adept at providing whatever service or product it sells that it meets demand right on time. Often, businesses instinctively know what the market is going to demand before it is demanded. You cannot teach this level of competence in a classroom, and you cannot learn it by reading a book. You may teach the concepts of such competency and learn the ideas surrounding them, but you must earn through years of effort and business experience how to execute consistently at this level. Even then, you will sometimes miss the mark.

Levels 3 and 4 are more about execution than they are about knowledge. Knowledge provides the foundation of competency, but flawless execution demonstrates that competency. Over the years, I have worked with many very intelligent people, some with degrees of higher learning and some without. I can say without hesitation that business success comes to a man or a woman who knows how to pull the trigger and not to a man or a woman who is educated but lacks the courage to act with boldness upon well laid plans. In a world that recognizes the doers and not the talkers, the doers are the only individuals who attain this ultimate level of competency.

*A dog is not considered a good dog because he is a good barker. A man is not considered a good man because he is a good talker.*

- Buddha

The attainment of this level of competency comes only after the payment of a high price of dedication and commitment while providing the highest quality product or service possible year after year. "Good enough" has never been "good enough" for the businesses that have paid these dues. They expect the best from themselves and analyze every detail when they succeed and when they fail. They are students of the game of business. These companies get up a little bit earlier in the morning and stay a little bit later in the evening than their competition. They know that to be the best in any endeavor they must earn everything they have and leave nothing on the table at the end of the day. Companies like this seem by first inspection to be "lucky." Instinct is not luck. Instinct is the result of hard work and a hell of a lot of effort. At Level 4, you have already earned the right to be there. Few companies pay their dues long enough and with enough precision and dedication to attain this level of competence.

Find that one thing you believe you can provide better than anyone else provides, dedicate yourself to knowing everything there is to know about it, and execute your delivery with a high level of quality year after year, and before you realize, it will be second nature.

## CONCLUDING THOUGHTS

There is no substitute for competence. Period. Life rewards the actions (or inaction) of each participant and no one is immune to this reality. Money will not exempt you from this law. Social standing will not exempt you from this law. A lack of money or social status does not excuse you from this law either. Both the rich and poor, the accomplished and derelict are all rewarded for their action. In a corporate setting, educational accomplishment, while impressive, does not excuse a lack of performance. In fact, it raises the expectation of excellence and high-quality results. Last year's big win that an executive or manager garnered for his or her company does not excuse poor performance this year.

When I was in the Navy, I had a Chief who told me upon check-in to his shop, "Chris, just remember, no matter how good of a job you do in this shop day after day, one 'oh-shit!' can wipe out a hundred 'atta-boys.'" I have never forgotten that lesson. It may seem unfair that one moment of incompetence or inattention to detail can delete a hundred accomplishments, but life is not fair. Life is unfair. Life is hard. Life rewards the competent who achieve great things regardless of the conditions in which they find themselves. Life does not reward intentions. The road to ruin is paved with the good intentions of the countless souls who travelled that way before. The road to victory is paved with the blood, sweat, tears, competence, and excellence of those who blazed the trail before you. The real world works that way. Get used to it.

# PRINCIPLE 7: CLEARLY DEFINE YOUR SCOPE AND ADHERE TO THE OBJECTIVES OF THE ORGANIZATIONAL PHILOSOPHY

*The last temptation is the greatest treason: to do the right deed for the wrong reason.*

- T. S. Eliot

The organization that desires to transition from or completely avoid a crisis management style of leadership in exchange for a focused management philosophy must learn how to train and hire project and program managers to lead different key divisions within the company. Executives with project management skills are focused on results and cost/benefit issues, and every decision they make is weighed by the benefit against the cost (read: *the risk*) to the organization. The lens of risk management colors every decision of the project manager or project leader. In this chapter, we are going to discuss the scope and objective of your organization as well as what a quality management mentality means to the organization. To crystallize this idea, think of scope and objectives more in terms of an overarching paradigm and culture than a finite initiative. While the scope and objectives may be well thought out and well written, they may be circumvented by the culture of the organization. As long as the leadership, management, and associates within your organization believe *"good enough is good enough,"* the organization will never make the leap from crisis management to project management and ultimately, the Quality Paradigm.

## SCOPE CREEP - HOW IT AFFECTS YOUR BUSINESS AND HOW TO ADDRESS IT

Scope creep can be a profit killer (and a shareholder and stakeholder's worst nightmare) if it is not actively managed. Once scope creep has set in, there is usually no way the business can meet budgets, meet deadlines, or produce an intended product or result. For those of you who are unfamiliar with the term "scope creep" as applied to project management circles, for our purposes it can be defined generally as small deviations from a stated project plan that ultimately necessitate other small changes *ad infinitum*. Over the years, I have heard some consultants and other business people offer the argument that scope creep is merely the normal process through which the buyer determines what he or she really wants. As a result, consultants and project managers often use this as an opportunity to up-sell the client with more products and services he or she probably does not need. The above argument ignores the fact that the buyer *initially agreed to what he said he wanted in the initial project plan and probably signed a contract as a result.* The determination of what the buyer "really wants" should have been done during the discovery and agreement phase. Often what happens is the consultant or project manager (or the executive leading a project) fails to properly control the initial phase (often referred to as the *initiation phase*) of the project because either he does not know the right questions to ask or fails to ask the right questions that will lead the buyer to determine what he wants.

Scope creep is another insidious and equally destructive manifestation that finds itself within the permanent structure of the organization, as opposed to a transient project with a set deliverable date. Often in small- to medium-sized businesses (and even in some international organizations) the scope, functionality, responsibilities, and interaction of departments and divisions will creep due to any number of different reasons. Ultimately, poor management and lack of control are generally to blame for this sort of internal scope creep. The term "responsibility creep" may be a more accurate description of this type of scope creep.

Many times an organization will have highly competent people in key positions, and these highly competent people will ultimately pull the weight of the completely incompetent people who also hold key positions. I can recall a situation such as this when incompetent leaders were never removed from a company because their incompetence was overlooked due to prior academic achievement. As a result, poor performance hobbled the organization, forcing it to hire multiple people to account for the underperformance of the key players, and the organization became bloated and disorganized. If you run into a situation where an executive of any type with any level of education or professional certification fails to perform his or her duties with excellence and then retreats behind academic letters (or past victories), it is probably best to let these people go. Your company cannot pay bills in excuses or intentions. The investors and Board of Directors do not receive their bonuses and dividends in the form of academic letters or excuses. Do not sacrifice what is profitable because of what is academically, professionally, or socially proper. In the real world, academic achievement and certifications only heightens the expectation of peak performance.

Understanding the vision of the organization is the bedrock of killing scope creep. In one or two sentences, your company must determine *what the organization does*. Determining this will define the soul of the company. Konosuke Matsushita began Matsushita Electric Industrial Company, Ltd. (so called until January 2008) in 1917 for the sole purpose of producing an electrical plug Matsushita had invented. For over 80 years, Matsushita Electric stayed true to its purpose of producing electronic and home appliance goods to the world. However, in 1990, a year after the founder's death, in an effort to match Sony's acquisition of CBS Records and Columbia Pictures, Matsushita acquired MCA Music and Universal Pictures. In what proved to be a marriage made in hell, Matsushita ultimately sold its MCA Music and Universal holdings five years later. The Japanese management and the management in California never saw eye to eye, and the merger was tenuous at best. Ultimately, Matsushita had gotten away from the business that had made them a world leader in so many different markets. Understanding the nature and vision of the organization can help to clarify which initiatives and strategic plans you should pursue and which you should not.

Another strategy for killing scope creep is identifying, defining, and adhering to organizational priorities and deliverables. *Is this the type of product a company like ours should be trying to produce?* If the answer is "no" or "I don't know," you have crept away from your foundational purposes. This is precisely what killed Lehman Brothers in 2008. Writing these priorities down and using these priorities for a guiding document for the performance of duties throughout the year can be a very powerful tool to maintaining positive control over your business. To clarify, you may make deviations, and you may add unforeseen additions to a project, but such changes must be justified by hard evidence in the form of costs versus benefits. Flying by the seat of your pants may work in movies, but the real world wants justifiable plans and ultimately positive results. For non-permanent projects, setting deadlines and milestones is the easiest and most basic way to lay a track for the manager to run on. While this may seem a bit basic to some, you would be amazed at the number of companies that set start dates but work their projects on open-ended timelines. Generally, companies like this never get anything done. You should set deadlines by when the customer (the market) needs the product or service in question. Why work a project for two years when the market needed the solution a year ago? I have actually seen this happen, and what is frustrating is the management was completely oblivious to these realities. Do not allow your company to fall into this trap because your company may not escape with its life.

## MACRO-SCOPE – GETTING THE BIG PICTURE RIGHT

In the world of sports, many times sportscasters refer to talented players and coaches as "students of the game." Seeing the big picture and learning how all of parts work together is the beginning of becoming a "student of the game" in the world of business. Looking at the big picture means you comprehend the operation of the entire machine and the purpose of each function along with how they work together to produce your product. Many times small business owners who become big business owners lose sight of how all of the pieces are supposed to work together and for what purpose. Running a business means leading the charge, and leading the charge means trusting the managers and directors to manage the minutia of the daily operations with a skillful hand. Too often business owners are stuck in the habit of wanting to be involved in the little things that make the company work in the same ways they were involved when the company was small. They miss doing the business of the business and many times end up micro-managing areas of the company on which they have no business focusing. If the manager you hired to manage business processes or departmental operations was competent enough to place into the senior management position, you must also leave them alone long enough to do the job. The problem is many business owners hate being business people – they love being entrepreneurs on the front lines. The transition between doing the work and managing the work can be difficult. The transition from managing the work to leading the organization can be even more challenging.

To illustrate, let me tell you a story:

> There was a man who owned some sheep. This shepherd loved his sheep more than anything else he loved. He devoted his entire life to supplying the needs of his flock, and as a result, the flock produced enough wool and goods to supply the needs of the shepherd and his family. Over the years, the man grew very wealthy, and his flocks grew so large that he was unable to care for all of the sheep the way he had always cared for them when there were but a few. Unfortunately, this led to some of these sheep wondering off and getting hurt, thieves stealing some of the sheep, and others becoming sick and dying. The shepherd knew he needed to hire some help, so he went to the local town and found some men of good repute who had helped other shepherds in the past and who were honest and hard working.
>
> After many months of working with these new men, the shepherd was unable to force himself to leave the men alone in the fields. Even though their work was

honest and true, he constantly looked after them and questioned their work. All the while, the sheep that the shepherd was supposed to look after were still wondering off, being stolen, and hurting themselves.

A few seasons came and went until the situation grew worse and the hired men came to the shepherd and told him the lands where the sheep graze were becoming unfertile and insufficient to support his flocks. They suggested he move the sheep from the current hills to other more fertile lands to the south so the unfertile lands could have time to recover. The shepherd replied sharply, "No! These are the lands my father and his father have cared for and owned for generations. This is how I have always raised my flocks. I know these lands, and I will never leave!" The hired men knew that without moving the flocks the sheep would begin to die, and with fewer sheep to tend, they would have to be let go. One by one over the coming months, the hired men left to work other flocks leaving the shepherd to tend his dying sheep. Eventually, only a few sheep remained, enough just for the shepherd to tend. The following spring season the rains did not come, and the fields did not produce their grass. Even the few sheep he did have left died.

Now, there was an industrious young shepherd living in the next town who heard about the man's difficulty and carefully observed his folly. When the shepherd's hired men left his fields and went to look for work with other flocks, this young shepherd quickly hired them. The young shepherd observed their work for a time before giving them charge over his flocks. After they earned his trust, the young master gave the hired men the full care of all of his flocks. As the men supplied the needs of the flocks, the flocks began to multiply across the land. The herds were so vast that one could hardly see the end of them from across the valley.

Having a keen eye the young shepherd knew the land

where he presently grazed the sheep could not sustain all of his flocks. Some of the elders in the town came to the young man and reminded him that these lands were the lands of his ancestors and that leaving these lands would break a tradition that had held for generations. The young man respectfully answered the elders by saying, "Honored fathers, what if our traditions have kept us from prospering further in the land where we have lived for so many years? What if these borders set by the hands of men around our great lands and that are meant to keep out invaders and outsiders have actually also *served to keep us in*? I say no; we must strike out and find new lands to work and new horizons to challenge. If we are to prosper, we must seek new lands. Please know esteemed men, my seeking new land does no dishonor to the lands and traditions of our ancestors or the work they have toiled these many years. There was a day when the land of our forefathers was once a new land to them as well."

Therefore, the young man set out on a journey to find flowing rivers and green pastures upon which he could raise his sheep. However, as the young shepherd set out he realized he was not sure exactly what to look for, so he went back to seek the counsel of his hired men. "What type of lands shall I search for that can sustain these many flocks?" he asked. The hired men replied, "Sir, we feel the answer to your question would best be made by asking the sheep what lands upon which they would like to graze and eat. Surely, it is they and not us who must prosper there." And so after much talking the young ruler had learned from the hired men exactly what these sheep ate and how they behaved in all conditions. Armed with this information, he set out again to find the lands necessary for his flocks to prosper. After many days of travel and seeing many different lands, the young shepherd finally found a green valley fed by streams of snowy run-off. The land was beautiful and open. It was the perfect land upon which to expand his herds. Quickly the man returned with his news and made plans to expand his flocks.

There are many lessons to learn from the story above. I will leave it to you to pull from the story the lessons you think would be applicable to you or to your situation. The ten lessons I would like to leave you with are these:

1. **The first shepherd did not fail because he was a poor shepherd (businessperson);** *he failed because he was a poor leader.* This shepherd failed in two specific ways. First, he failed to *lead* the hired men (managers); instead, he micro-managed them. Secondly, he failed to look for new opportunities for his flocks because he was focused on how things had always *been* done and not upon how things should be done *now*. Poor leaders are insecure, untrusting, and change-resistant. Notice, the man never stopped being a good shepherd, he simply never made the leap to being a good leader, and that ultimately caused him to fail in shepherding.

2. **The micro-management of the first shepherd took away his time and attention from his own responsibilities, and the sheep he was responsible to care for suffered because of it.** If you are micro managing your staff, you cannot be doing *your* job. If you have the free time to micro-manage your management and your personal work does not suffer, that means you really do not have enough to do to justify needing managers in the first place. If you believe in the idea that if you want something done right you have to do it yourself, you are telling everyone around you that the only right way is your way and that you are the only one on the team capable enough to actually do a job properly. It tells your team that you do not think they are competent or capable of doing the job you hired them to perform. Communicating this type of message is a sure fire way to lose good people and replace them with under achievers that require micro-management (this is a waste of good resources). When tempted to micro-manage a situation or a person, ask yourself two

questions: (1) Is he or she being efficient, and (2) Is he or she completing the task within satisfactory standards? There is only one way to do anything, and that is *the right way*, even if it is not necessarily your way.

3. **The first shepherd did not listen to his men who spent their days in the trenches.** When your management team brings issues to your attention, you need to carefully assess and listen to what they are saying. I have a few rules I lay down with clients and subordinates to facilitate this. First, if you are going to raise a concern, bring quantifiable or some other conclusive data to support the concern. Second, if you are going to raise a concern, bring at least two or three solid solutions. This method enables the suspected root cause and possible solutions to be brought to the manager's attention at the same time and eliminates the manager and staff from complaining at you for no particular reason.

4. **The first shepherd refused to change with the current conditions because of how the lands and sheep had always been managed before.** I have heard many different variations of this paradigm, but generally, it boils down to an idea that says, "That's not how we used to do it" or the ever famous and equally annoying, "I remember when I was doing your job we used to…" Unless you are pointing out past procedure for education's sake or taking a stroll down memory lane, do not get caught in this trap. How you used to do something is immaterial because that was then, and this is now. The winds have shifted, and both the opportunities and challenges of today are probably different from yesterday. When you were doing <fill in the blank> the company probably looked a whole lot different, and the marketplace probably did too. Do not insult your people through belittling their hard work by equating what you did when the company had five clients and what they do now that the company

has 5,000 clients. Nothing you did then even remotely compares to the job they do now. Save the nostalgic stories for Christmas dinner.

5. **The hired men did not leave the sheep;** *they left the shepherd.* People will leave your organization because of *your* leadership or the leadership of your managers. *People leave poor relationships and rarely leave due to differences with the corporate philosophy of a company.* This is why human resource management is so important and why every organization needs to invest heavily into training leaders to lead, managers to manage, and workers to work. Resist the urge to listen to the popular organizational growth nonsense about every person in the organization becoming a leader in order to maximize growth. It is just not true; it creates a huge headache when everyone tries to lead and proves to be discouraging to those who are not cut out for leadership. Not everyone is capable of becoming a leader, and that is ok. I have said it before, and I will say it again – I do not want the assemblyman on the line trying to be a leader; *I want him trying to be the best damn assemblyman he can become before he retires.* If he becomes a manager, I want him to manage as Shakespeare wrote plays, and if he ever becomes an executive leader, then I want him to lead like his livelihood depends on it – because it does.

6. **The young shepherd was wise and observed the missteps of the other shepherd and then applied the principles he learned to his own business.** Leaders are learners. There are always things you can improve within your leadership style. Situations and conditions always change, and if you are unwilling or unable to adapt to the changes that face your company, you are going to fail. Every year successful businesses reassess their business strategy and their human resources to make sure they have the right people in the right positions doing the right things to assure continued

growth and future success. Successful organizations learn from other players in the marketplace as well as the companies they compete against for market share. Knowledge is defined by learning from your own successes and mistakes. Wisdom is defined as learning from other people's successes and mistakes. It takes both knowledge *and* wisdom to manage a business successfully.

7. **The young shepherd hired talent he knew was competent and gave them the opportunity to demonstrate that competency.** Talented people flow toward companies that will utilize their abilities and unique skill sets and pay them what they are worth. Part of utilizing talented people is giving them opportunities to overcome challenges and to demonstrate their competence. Not only will this foster the manager's confidence in the hired talent, but it also allows them to feel comfortable in their role. Additionally, the they will usually find a sense of personal pride and satisfaction in their work. These benefits are essential to maintaining top talent within your company and attracting new talent as the organization grows.

8. **The young shepherd forecasted conditions that would directly affect his flocks BEFORE these conditions became a challenge.** In chess, the winner is usually the player who thinks more steps ahead than his or her opponent does. For example, if I think two steps ahead and you think four steps ahead, you are most likely going to win every time. The global marketplace that exists today requires leaders and managers to think in three or four dimensions. What are the cause and effect issues directly related to your company's strategy? What are the cause and effect issues directly related to your competition's strategy? What effect will the marketplace and consumer behavior have on what goods and services your company provides

(and that of your competition)? The Quality Paradigm requires the executive management to think several steps ahead of the organization's current position in the market. If you take business day by day with no forecast regarding the driving forces in your market, you will not last long at all.

9. **The young shepherd challenged the paradigm of the establishment and employed courage to speak candidly about challenges and practices that have served to hinder growth.** This is not your daddy's marketplace, and the opportunities afforded to your business right now may require you to challenge key assumptions or corporate culture in order to capture them. The companies gaining market share are the companies that have positioned themselves within the market to provide customers exactly what they want when they want it. This is what drives the goal of total customer satisfaction. Sacred cows are showstoppers in today's world of business (and I don't mean the song and dance type of showstoppers). Shareholders and consumers demand the very best and highest output from the companies in which they invest or with whom they do business. By sacred cows, I mean anyone or anything that hinders growth and opportunity for your business. Sacred cows take the form of executives and managers, corporate cultures, leadership paradigms, management paradigms, resource management and investment philosophies, or the like. Outside of ethical and guiding principles (which are immutable), everything can be challenged in a quality-focused organization.

10. **The young shepherd consulted the talented men who worked for him and gathered information before making key decisions concerning future strategy and growth.** Notice in the story that the talented men advised the young shepherd to ask, "...the sheep what lands upon which they would like to graze and

eat" because "it is they and not us who must prosper there." Customer satisfaction begins with asking the customers what they desire, studying their behaviors, anticipating what they will want or need in the future, and positioning the company internally and in the marketplace to provide those things at the exact time it is needed. The only way to mine this information is to collect data from the people within the organization who are in direct contact with the customers. Who better to glean important information from than the customers themselves and the people who ensure they are completely satisfied? Communicate constantly with the people within the organization about customer desires, and set up systems to collect this data directly from customers as well. You can never have too much of this information. I will leave you with a word of caution when collecting data, though. The data must be organized, functional, and utilized. I once worked with a company that collected thousands of feedbacks and comments from customers, and the management and executive leadership never read any of the reports with any regularity. Consequently, the organization failed to address key concerns clients had with the business, and the business eventually stagnated, experienced flat growth (read: *no growth*), and ultimately began to decline.

## MICRO-SCOPE – SWEAT THE SMALL STUFF; IT DETERMINES THE BIG STUFF

The little cycles and tendencies within your company *always* determine the big cycles and tendencies within your company. Ultimately, this will affect your customers in some way, whether they realize it or not. The little things are of monumental importance. To illustrate this fact, let us say you were navigating a ship and accidentally made a 1° deviation from your present course; in 300 miles you would be 5.25 miles (27,720 feet) away from your intended destination. The same principle holds true in business.

Three reasons people miss the details include:

1. **Carelessness due to a lack of skills or familiarity:** Many times people miss details because they lack the proper skill set to know what to look for in the first place or because they are unfamiliar with what a process should look like when it is completed. Overestimating the competence of staff members can set your company or department up for failure and serve to ruin an otherwise promising member of your team. During my time in the Navy, I supervised my squadron's flight-line division. My division was responsible for the safety of all of our aircraft (over $300 million worth), which included all of the aircraft support equipment and the launching and recovering of aircraft. Anytime there was a mishap or mistake, one of the very first steps in the investigation was to determine the training of the sailor involved and to ensure he or she had the proper qualifications to perform the evolution that caused the mishap. Once the investigators established the qualifications, they analyzed the experience level of the personnel involved. Everything was reviewed, from environmental hazards to the details of the pre-evolution briefing. Anytime there is a mishap in the aviation industry, it is usually a string of small deviations over a period of time that all align properly to produce an accident. The same principle is true in your business as well. Very rarely will a problem arise because of a catastrophic unforeseen failure. Usually problems arise from missing several small details over the course of an evolution.

2. **Familiarity breeds contempt:** For those employees who have been a part of your organization for an extended period of time, a danger lurks in familiarity. While not knowing what a process or outcome should look like can cause problems, an over-familiarization with process can cause an equal amount of problems. To complicate matters, the personnel who make these kinds of mistakes are usually your star players. This

fact makes holding them accountable even more difficult for some managers. Familiarity with a process often leads to the temptation to cut corners and to shortcut steps in the process. I see this all of the time in my work in the quality community. While performing maintenance and flight duties as an Aircrewman in the Navy, I was a slave to my checklist. The reason for this was to address the danger in unfamiliarity and over-familiarity by setting a standard process to follow at each stage of an evolution. Checklists never have the potential to forget because they are set in stone and repeatable. The only chance for deviation from the standard is if the personnel deviate from the individual steps laid out to accomplish a process. Quality assurance always audits against a set standard, and it is this standard that assures a person familiar with a process always produces a repeatable and predictable outcome.

3.  **Lack of work ethic:** Thomas Edison once quipped, "We often miss opportunity because it's dressed in overalls and looks like work." Work ethic is one of those intangibles that are very difficult to coach and develop. People who lack work ethic often perform the minimum amount of work required to keep their jobs and expect the highest possible compensation. Performing the minimum all but guarantees that details will be missed in a process. I believe the number one reason people with low work ethic are hired by companies is that the hiring process for finding talent lacks the proper mechanisms to weed out poor performers. If you have a constant breakdown in a certain function of your business, I would review all of the personnel in the department and make sure everyone has the work ethic required to work for your company. By setting high standards of work ethic within your company, a sense of *esprit de corps* and internal accountability will begin to develop, and workers will begin to take ownership and pride in their personal output. People

who become proud of their work focus on details, are more productive, and do not tolerate poor work ethic from themselves or from others.

Focusing on the small stuff does not mean allowing it to mesmerize you so that you take your eyes off the big picture. The big picture and the details all have to be kept in their proper perspectives. As the executive manager or leader, you have to be aware of many things at the same time. While there are times this will seem overwhelming, over time you will learn what works for you and customize your leadership and management styles to accommodate these tasks. Situational awareness allows you to be aware of what needs your attention and what does not. One thing is certain: you must be fully engaged in the projects and processes of your organization, or else they will spin out of your control when you least expect them to.

## TELE-SCOPE – LOOKING TO THE FUTURE AND PLANNING FOR TOMORROW

When I was a boy (and even at times when I became an adult), I dreamed of going to the final frontier and rocketing into space to visit the stars. One year for Christmas, I received a telescope from my parents and stayed up many nights thereafter staring at the stars in wonder. For me, the stars gave me hope that the future could be bright and that even when things seemed to be bad there was always hope for tomorrow. Tomorrow matters because you are destined to spend the rest of your life there. If tomorrow never comes, it becomes a moot point anyway; *so plan for it.* When I was a manager very early in my career, the owner of the company I worked for came to me one day and told me, *"Piss Poor Planning Produces Piss Poor Performance."* He called it the Law of the Seven P's. Over the course of my career, I have heard this same principle referred to in many different ways, but the message is always the same; plan for the future. Below I have outlined some questions to ask when considering the future and determining what course to set for your organization. Some of the questions that should be included in any strategic planning effort are:

- If you could paint the perfect picture, what would the ideal outcome for the business look like this year?
- What obstacles can you readily identify that you would

have to deal with immediately in order to achieve these outcomes?

- What assets can you readily identify that you would have to employ or capitalize on in order to achieve these outcomes?
- What are the results you want to see accomplished?
- Why are you trying to accomplish these results this year? Do they play a role in a bigger strategic picture?
- What is the cost/benefit trade-off, and ultimately what is your Return on Investment (ROI) going to be? Is this ROI acceptable, and is the risk to achieve this within your comfort range?
- What is your unique selling proposition (USP), and how do these objectives support this end?
- Will these objectives help improve market share?

As discussed previously, objectives are the outcomes that the organization wants to achieve within a certain period of time and under certain conditions. Establishing clear and concise objectives involves asking the right questions and answering these questions honestly.

## ESTABLISHING THE METRICS OF OBJECTIVES

Some would say that the Total Quality Management methodology (developed by Deming) and the Management By Objectives methodology (largely developed by Drucker) are at odds and irreconcilable. For 30 years, the Management By Objectives (MBO) philosophy ruled the day in American business. Deming and his consultative work with the Japanese countered the American model during the post World War II rebuilding effort in Japan during that same period. By the 1980s, the Japanese had begun to far outperform their American counterparts, which gave rise to the interest of American business community in the Total Quality Management (TQM) methodology and initiatives such as 5S and Six Sigma, two of the many examples. The result was a migration in the 1990s away from the MBO methodology of the previous 30 years. As often is the case when drastically different philosophies are compared, camps began to arise and create an "either/or" conversation among quality and management professionals. As the economy of the 21st century has begun to develop and take shape, the "either/or" discussion of management philosophy has begun to take a new direction. It is my opinion, as well as the opinion of others, that the combination of the very best of both philosophies can produce far better results than ever imagined.

While Deming was wholly against managing by goals, objectives, and personal evaluation, American business has proven through results that the philosophy is sound and works well. In the same way, businesses have proven that Deming's TQM philosophy also works well and provides results. My inclusion of the SMART process of establishing objectives, advocated in Drucker's MBO philosophy, is an extension of my belief that both philosophies have merit and can serve as a positive foundation upon which to manage any enterprise. Below is one of the many variations of the SMART process of developing objectives. Companies widely use this easy to remember mnemonic that outlines the specific steps involved in creating objectives for projects or processes.

Objectives must be:
1. **Specific:** Specificity is the foundation of achieving a strong set of objectives for an organization or a project. Objectives cannot be vague or nebulas because there would be no way to quantify, focus, or properly resource the strategy. Specificity provides purpose and a rallying point around which the management can train, motivate, and organize the achievement of work. The power of focus enables all of the players on the field to know their position and accomplish their jobs.

2. **Measurable:** Objectives must be measurable so you may track progress and navigate properly the course of the organization or project. *Remember this rule: If you cannot measure it, you cannot properly manage it.* Management requires a purposed direction toward some end (generally referred to as a goal). The vision of the executive leadership lays out goals of the

organization, and the expression of overall strategy is through objectives. If a company cannot measure these objectives or demonstrate quantitatively the work of the team, there will be no way to know whether they are making any progress, and the team will be unstable. The last thing in the world a manager wants to develop within his company or department is a "why are we here" mentality. Measurable objectives will eliminate this threat.

3. **Actionable:** The best-laid plans are useless unless you are actually able to do them. Be very careful not to fall into the trap of devising an elaborate plan of action without the ability to perform. You do not get points for the game plan; you get points for executing the game plan and scoring points. Remember, life rewards action, which is why talk is cheap; the supply of talking and planning is always greater than the demand. Do you have the financial resources to complete the project or achieve stated goals? Do you have the proper players on the field to accomplish the tasks required to complete the objectives? Do your managers and staff have the skill set required to accomplish the objectives? Just because you have a sales force does not mean you have sales. Can the sales force sell at a rate that keeps up with the measurable milestones set out in the strategic plan? Is your product or service sellable to the number of people required to achieve the objectives? Are there any market conditions that would be prohibitive to achieving these objectives? Can your managers manage a department with a budget of $10 million when the most they have been able to manage successfully in the past is $2 million, or will they feel overmatched and falter under the stress? Perception is not reality. Substance is reality. What is really going on? Is this plan feasible?

4. **Resourced properly:** Underfunding is arguably the number one killer of businesses and projects. If the

achievement of objectives becomes impossible or improbable because they are underfunded, it matters little whether or not you have the physical ability to achieve the objectives. All of the pieces of the puzzle have to be in place in order to achieve the goals and objectives. Be cautious of over-funding businesses and projects as well. Having too much money available often leads to spending resources in ways that are not critical to the achievement of the stated purposes. Often this leads to the accumulation of expenses that linger after the project is closed or the objectives met. Be sure to do a cost/benefit analysis on every stage of the plan and determine with fair accuracy how much funding the project or objectives will require, and fund only that amount. Years ago, I owned a real estate investment firm that focused on buying distressed properties, rehabilitating them, and holding them as a long-term investment. We treated every house as an individual project and only dispersed the funding required to meet our company's specifications for repairs on the project. We determined that a 2,500 ft$^2$ house would cost $x$ amount of dollars to repair, only bid on properties that fit this profile, and picked up properties at a reasonable percentage below loan value. In all of our investments, these controls allowed our company never to run over budget or to over-leverage ourselves. In the same way, your company must make sure the funding required to meet the objectives is precisely the funding it provides – no more and no less.

5. **Time-bound:** Deadlines are the banks that cause the river to flow. A river without banks is not a river at all; it is a stagnant swamp. Deadlines allow the processes to move forward and for the completion of objectives dependent upon one another at the proper times to execute the game plan. Adhering to deadlines is of equal importance to setting the deadline itself. Who cares how many deadlines have been set if you are

going to blow right through them like they did not exist? Very stringent consequences should be set for missing deadlines due to any reason other than something absolutely out of the knowledge or control of the organization. Every deadline missed is money spent that was not allocated for the completion of the objective. Deadlines only work when the managers take a no-excuses approach to accomplishing organizational objectives. When I was in the United States Navy, we had a *no-excuses* approach to making sure our aircraft were "mission capable" when the time came for the aircraft to fly. Mission completion is very important to the military, and short of a catastrophic failure of an aircraft, there are no excuses for the planes not to meet their mission tasking. Our skipper did not want to hear excuses; he just wanted to see planes in the sky. You must embrace this same mentality with moving forward and accomplishing your company's objectives.

## CONCLUDING THOUGHTS

The intention of this chapter was to address the importance of viewing the big picture, paying attention to the details, and positioning your company to capitalize on future opportunities. Focusing on the scope and objectives of your business is paramount to the short-term and long-term viability of your growing business. The major hazards that trip up managers and business leaders usually have something to do with far sightedness, near sightedness, or missing opportunities due to poor positioning. Setting SMART objectives provides a track on which your business or department to run.

As discussed to above, there has been much discussion and opposing points of view concerning the compatibility of TQM and MBO philosophies. History shows that utilizing a combination of both philosophies to effectively control market share and build an effective company that provides total customer satisfaction is not only realistic but also effective. To be effective in the economy of the 21st century, companies must mine both MBO and TQM philosophies for the best practices in each and then combine these ideas in such a way to produce the most efficient management process possible. What was missing from the MBO philosophy of the past was a focus and commitment to lean quality during production. "Doing things right" does not mean you are *doing the right things*. There is no point to climbing ladders leaning against wrong walls. Conversely, producing quality products makes no difference if your organization suffers from dysfunction and wrong market placement. While these generalizations are surely oversimplified, they still serve well enough to highlight the major detractors from each philosophy. Doing the right things at the highest possible quality and having a crystallized plan for its achievement should be the goal of every manager and executive in small and medium sized businesses.

# PRINCIPLE 8: RESPONSIBILITY, AUTHORITY, AND RESOURCES – FINALLY, A *MÉNAGE À TROIS* THAT WORKS

*If you don't drive your business, you will be driven out of business.*

- BC Forbes

Every company needs to have people who have been properly empowered to produce results for their company. Take the most competent and educated leader or manager and put that person in a situation where he or she is provided undefined responsibilities, no authorities, and limited resources, and I will show you a project or company that is headed for failure. Yet this common-sense conclusion escapes many otherwise intelligent and competent businesspeople. Companies are consistently mismanaged and underfunded. In this chapter, we are going to look at the proper balance that you need to strike between responsibility, authority, and resources. We will also define responsibility; discover what true authority (otherwise known as *power*) is, where it comes from, and how giving it away is the only way to have more of it; and look at financial and human capital issues and some guiding principles on how to manage such resources properly.

# RESPONSIBILITIES
## *The Myth of Fault*

Some people naturally avoid responsibility like the plague. Every organization has people who, for one reason or another, cannot seem to own any of their decisions or take responsibility for the failures of their departments. Many of these types of people are ruled by fear. Leadership and management of meaningful and integral business functions are *impossible* for the person driven by fear. In fact, the very basics of success (however you choose to define it) are impossible to achieve with a fearful disposition. Irrational or irresponsible acts of commission or omission will dismantle whatever progress you make toward the achievement of an objective. I included acts of omission because fearful people generally shrink back when faced with the hard decisions. For your business to survive, you must overcome this fear and make sure no one in any senior management position suffers from this state. This is a prime example of why a good vetting system is worth its weight in gold (literally) and will save your business from serious pain down the road.

When my children were very young, I began to preach to them about *the myth of fault*. The myth of fault says that when negative things happen or when the fortunes of life turn against you, it does not matter whose fault it is; all that matters is who is going to take responsibility for it and move forward. Ultimately, there is no one other than *you* who is responsible *for you or your reactions* to the challenges of life. In the context of personal accountability, there is no such thing as fault; all that exists is responsibility. Seeing situations accurately, knowing your role in the situation, and taking personal ownership of these roles are the foundation of being a responsible leader. Successful leaders have a specific trait called situational awareness. I taught my daughters very early that the pain caused by the consequences of blaming outside conditions is always greater in the long term than the initial discomfort of squaring their shoulders, looking the issue straight in the eye, and taking responsibility. Sometimes courage is physically and emotionally painful, but the rewards always outweigh the discomfort, whether in principle, in character, or in physical means.

## Personal

Taking personal responsibility for your life and your decisions is the first step to establishing personal leadership. America is facing a catastrophic vacuum of personal accountability resulting in social dysfunction, financial irresponsibility, and a general dissatisfaction with life. Many principle-centered leaders have been overwhelmed by the tide of entitlement-minded leaders who believe in providing minimum benefit for maximum compensation. This is due in large part to the fact that Americans have not been taught to take ownership for their lives for over a generation. If you are different, want to succeed, and earnestly desire to see your company succeed, you have to come to the realization that *there are no free lunches in this world.*

- No one is going to chase you down and teach you what you need to know to succeed.
- No one is going to pay your bills for you.
- No one is going to make those phone calls you were supposed to make.
- No one is going to raise your kids for you.
- No one is going to finish that degree for you.
- No one is going to write that book for you.
- No one is going to mail that letter for you.
- No one is going to tell your children how proud you are of them.
- No one is going to teach your kids personal responsibility and character for you.
- No one is going to love your spouse for you, and if someone does, you will be without a spouse soon anyway.
- No one is going to pursue your dreams for you.
- No one is going to live your life for you.
- It is your life. Live it. Stop looking for the meaning *of* life and ***start putting meaning in life.*** *The meaning is what you make it.*

Business people have been fooled into believing that working hard is not as wise as working smart. I am sure you have heard the popular maxim that goes, "Work smarter, not harder." Perhaps you have even said it yourself. Without proper context, the maxim is incorrect. Working smart is simply an admonition to organize processes and plans, while working hard should never be in question. It is not an either/or proposition, even though the maxim presents it that way. Every day is a gift, and everyday deserves 100% of your efforts and your attention. If you must have a maxim by which to live: *Work hard, smartly*.

You have one shot at this life, and either you decide to make the most of it, or you will find nothing of any lasting value and little satisfaction. No one is responsible for you except *you*. Life does not reward excuses for failure or excuses for poor performance with positive results. Life rewards action, either good or bad. For every action, there is a consequence, and for every consequence, there are a new set of circumstances and new decisions. Leadership starts in the mind with a decision to not go a day more or one step farther without owning every thought, every decision, and every action. Thoughts, decisions, and actions can sometimes lead to poor thinking, bad decisions, and undesirable consequences, but they can also lead to focused and critical thinking, smart decisions, and intended consequences.

Failure is not a risk you need to fear because the process of achieving your goals does not end with failure. It begins with failure. The process to achieving your goals never ends because life's journey only ends when you have drawn your last breathe. That said, failure is not an option; *it is a requirement*. If you never fail, you will never learn what works and what does not. The disconnect with many people is that once they have learned what works, they choose to continue in their folly instead. Personal leadership requires you to put the shovel down once you realize you have fallen into the hole and get busy climbing out.

## Corporate

Leadership and management begin on personal plains and expand outwardly to leading and managing others. If you are unable to lead or manage yourself, you will be unable to effectively lead or manage anyone else. Early in my career, I used to travel and teach leadership and personal growth. Something I learned from all of my travels is people are fixated with the idea of being "a leader" and often look down on those who are "just managers." This adolescent view of leadership and management always struck me as curious because otherwise intelligent and thoughtful individuals generally held it. I believe this myopic viewpoint of leadership is perpetuated thoughtlessly because Americans love a winner. It is in our blood. We are taught from a young age that second place is simply the first loser, and nobody wants to be *that* guy, even though we all know somebody inevitably always is. Many American small business people believe that winners are leaders and leaders are winners. To be a manager is to be second best, a sort of sub-par leader who could not hack it at the top so he or she was somehow forced to work for the "real" leaders. Or possibly the manager is simply on his or her way up to the top and working on becoming a leader one day when he or she has achieved some form of leadership enlightenment. *Nothing could be farther from the truth.*

While no one would disagree that leaders are called upon to lead and managers are called upon to manage, I would remind you that all leaders manage and all managers lead. The leader/manager interchange is a "we" model. For example, when I was in the Navy, I was a part of an aircrew that was called upon to operate as a team. Our plane carried over 20 different aircrew personnel with different jobs and objectives tethered together by one common mission. Clearly, each of us was at a different rank (some higher, some lower), but when the wheels were off of the ground and the mission was being executed, we operated as a team and relied upon the skill sets and expertise of the other members of the team regardless of their rank because they had earned the right to be on that plane through extensive training and dedication. Incompetence was unacceptable from anyone on the team regardless of rank, and we each held the other members accountable. If you failed your crew, you would run the risk of being removed from flight-status because you were deemed unreliable and therefore unsafe. Failing to lead when leadership is required or failing to manage when management is required will destabilize your company and possibly cause its demise.

The leadership style displayed by a leader in an organizational environment is usually an extension of his or her personal leadership style. Organizations invariably become reflections of the leaders who lead them. Over time the majority of your organizational dysfunction will probably be a reflection of the dysfunction in your leadership's personal habits and tendencies. Organizations are made up of people just like an organism is made up of cells. If some of these people within your organization have poor personal habits that have translated into poor leadership habits, what will develop is a sort of corporate cancer that generally you cannot cure unless you cut it out. Organizational leaders must be accountable for the results of the organizations. There are no excuses for poor performance if your leadership has failed to address key organizational objectives and take prudent action. Your company cannot pay dividends in excuses. If your company is to move forward and establish itself as a marketplace leader, you must put away excuses and touchy-feely politically correct leadership and get back to expecting results from yourself first and then your leadership and management team. Performance pays in profits. Period.

The responsibility of the leadership and the management is to expect production and results from themselves first and then the rest of the organization. Every leader and manager within the company must know without any shadow of doubt that missing deadlines is not tolerable; shattering budgets with run-away cost overruns is never acceptable; missing profitability projections by double-digit error margins is going to cost someone their job if the error was due to incompetence. By tooling your company to accommodate the slowest man, you allow the slowest man to hobble the whole company by incompetence. The ingredient that enables great businesses to be great is the great people who work for them. These people have the responsibility to produce positive results and more times than not they rise to the occasion and deliver.

## AUTHORITY
### *Power*

Power is the ability to command a controlling influence upon oneself and upon others. Power is the source of all progress and work that humanity has ever achieved and will ever undertake in the future. Personal power is the ability to control the mind and body and accomplish intended goals and objectives when outside influences press against you to impede your progress. Powerful people are inherently disciplined in the areas where they are powerful. However, this power does not necessarily spill over into other areas of a person's life. An example of this dynamic can be seen in people who are successful and wield great power professionally but have absolutely no power in keeping a healthy physical condition or healthy interpersonal relationships. Often powerful people and powerful organizations are snared by the folly of believing power in one area is power in all areas. Personal power is not omnipotent; it is limited by our personal capacities and guided by our habits.

Power is the currency of life and is in constant motion between people and organizations. Power is abundant. Everyone has power readily available, yet power is scarcely found because very few people know how to access the power available to them and regulate the power they give to others. This is due in large part to a lack of understanding of what power truly is, who has it, and who is worthy to have it. Power can inspire the most timid or oppressed of people to refuse to go to the back of the bus. Power can inspire masses of people to push back against tyranny and terror. Power can also be used to crush the spirits of children. Power can control the weak and vulnerable. Power can bring hope and destruction with the same sweeping force. Authority is not a toy and should never be entrusted in large amounts to the juvenile or the incompetent.

Ultimately, power flows in two directions: toward you and away from you. The power you have over yourself is inherent and comes from your personal view and attitude about yourself. The power others have over you is only as much as you have chosen to give to them. The power others possess over you ultimately comes by your permission. The power you have with others is only as much as they have chosen to give to you. Your power with others comes from them whether they realize it or not. While control over others can always be taken by force, cooperative and productive power with others is by permission.

For example, examine the relationship between children and parents. Parents control a child's food, clothing, housing, security, entertainment, and anything else that pertains to life. The parent has complete control. As the child grows and begins to assert himself, the parent begins to lose control over the mind of the child, and conflict often results. The parent censures privileges to control behaviors, and the child must decide whether to obey or to disobey. This obedience or disobedience from the child is the act of giving or withholding power from the parent. Ultimately, if the child willfully disobeys, he is telling the parent that she has no power to control his actions regardless of what physical measures the parent may pursue. The child has control, and the parent is forced to manage the child at the lowest level of management: brute force. If this scenario was different and the child decided to obey the parent, he would be extending his permission for the parent to have power.

Useful power with others is always earned. If leaders and managers do not earn the right to exercise power beyond positional authority, they will ultimately fail to produce any lasting change or effectual results.

### *Whence Cometh Power?*

Power comes from two sources: *commission and permission.* If you are in senior management or ownership, the bestowal of power is by your clients and customers. The permission of power comes from peers and subordinates within the organization. Power not commissioned by senior leadership and merely assumed by a person supported by peers and subordinates is called *mutiny,* and such action will certainly have you looking for other employment (I have actually witnessed this while doing work with a Fortune 500 company). Power conferred by superiors but rejected by those subordinate to them will result in tyranny of management, poor performance, and process inefficiency. The subordinate people will sabotage any attempt by the leader to lead or manage, and generally, the situation will digress to gridlock. Both commission and permission must be present for a leader to lead effectively and a manager to manage efficiently.

Leadership by commission is very important to the health of an organization, specifically in the commissioning of highly skilled and competent management. Quality initiatives must begin with commissioning high quality individuals with a passion for doing the right things right, at the right time, on time, and at or below budget. While this is a pretty tall order, successful companies all over the world manage to pull it off every day. The key to establishing a success-minded quality culture is the insertion of high quality component personnel into a well-planned process. Quality starts at the top and filters downward. An army of highly proficient and competent soldiers will find defeat when led by an incompetent General and incompetent Lieutenants. Incompetent leaders do not know how to hire competent personnel because either they do not know what to look for or they become intimidated by it when they do find it.

Any quality initiative needs to begin by looking in the mirror and taking an honest self-appraisal of your own skill and competence levels. I call this the "ugly baby" test. Nobody wants to admit their baby is ugly anymore than they want to admit they are incompetent, but if you ever hope to overcome personal ugliness, you need to embrace the facts and make changes. Is the company ugly because your leadership is ugly? It bears thinking about. Next, you need to ensure that every person on your staff is of the highest quality you can afford now. How ugly is their baby? What are their competencies and skill sets? Can they take your organization where you need it to go to achieve your goals and objectives? Once the leadership and management are in place, the process can be executed with excellence. Poor execution and incompetence are capital crimes in quality circles and should be capital crimes in your organization, as well. If you turn a blind eye to incompetence or poor performance in the management and leadership of your company, you will feed an epidemic of problems in staff members.

Leadership by permission is also of equal importance to leading a quality-focused organization. If the people within the organization do not buy into what you are doing, they will resist, some overtly and some covertly. It is unwise to expect the best from subordinates and not demonstrate that same level of commitment to excellence yourself. Earlier I used the example of a parent/child relationship to demonstrate how others give power to the leader. I alluded to the idea that the earning of power comes before the granting of permission for the leader to lead. Parents who wait until a child is a teenager to begin investing into their parental relationships are out of luck. It becomes extremely difficult (nigh impossible) to earn the right to have any sort of power in that relationship. When my own children were born I made the decision that I would never lie to them about things like the Easter Bunny, Santa Claus, the Tooth Fairy, where babies came from (I avoided that one as long as I could), drugs, alcohol, or anything they would ever think to ask about. I kept my girls informed of details and information they needed to have at the time they needed it, and I never misdirected them about the facts of situations. Additionally, I held myself accountable to apologize for own my mistakes when I would speak crossly at them inappropriately, misjudged situations, or hurt their feelings unintentionally. I was always careful to follow through with administering the consequences of breaking the rules. I was firm, but I was fair. My daughters always knew they could count on me when I gave my word to them. This transparency and authenticity allowed me to earn the permission to speak into their lives. Every day they saw that the same man who was their father at home was the same businessperson in the office or the same coach on the field.

The first step to managing and leading by permission is walking before the people transparent and authentic. The rules for you are the rules for them. The consequences for you are the consequences for them. The failures of the organization are yours and yours alone. The victories of the organization are the victories of the team. These things earn the permission for the leader and the manager to do their jobs and build a quality team.

## *Balancing Power*

*Being powerful is like being a lady. If you have to tell people you are; you aren't.*

- Margaret Thatcher

Equilibrium in leadership and management responsibilities is as important as the equilibrium between your personal life and professional career. Each year hundreds, if not thousands of books are published to address the problem of balance. I will not attempt to solve this dilemma here in this short space; however, I would like to offer up some key information that may help you to strike that balance.

As I have had the opportunity to travel the world and meet

people and speak to business and civic leaders from all four corners of the United States, I have noticed that the most well respected and authentically successful individuals were those who were fiercely competitive yet not petulant and unmerciful. They were focused yet not to the exclusion of the well-being of their staff, co-workers, and partners. In almost every situation, I found these people to have both feet firmly planted on the ground, and many had no more respect for themselves than they had earned. All were philanthropic. Each was very savvy about matters of finance and matters directly relating to their respective industries. They stayed away from extremes and looked for a center within themselves that gave them a confident poise. It was from this seat of poise that they projected their power to perform whatever genius they had to offer the world. Each was passionate about their work and their businesses, but each controlled this passion and focused its energy on getting things done.

If you fail to find a balance in your corporate culture, you will burn your people out, or the company will be bloated and inefficient. Burn-out is the most classic symptom of imbalance I can think of. When tasking leaves no room for *esprit de corps* and the building of a cohesive team is hampered by a "Why are we here?" mood, it is a sure bet there is a balance problem. A balanced leader has a balanced company – it is that simple. If your organization is in a state of imbalance, look in the mirror, and analyze whether or not your personal habits and leadership style lack balance.

The opposite of burn-out is lethargy, otherwise known as corporate bloat. Corporate bloat is commonly due to a lack of performance from personnel that requires the hire of several people to account for this loss of productivity. At some point, the leadership failed to bring the management into balance by disciplining poor performance immediately. You cannot ignore poor performance. By refusing to discipline poor performance, you are rewarding it and giving it fuel to grow. Once poor performance finds acceptance (overtly or passively), the poor performer will serve as an example to peers and subordinates that the senior leadership is soft on these issues. This signal often leads to a massive decrease in productivity and then more bloating.

## *Delegating Authority*

I was at a dinner party in the Seattle area being held by the local Chamber of Commerce when I had the opportunity to speak with one of the wealthier real estate investors in the area. During the course of our conversation, I asked him to what key factor he most attributed his success and to what key factor he attributed missteps along the way. He smiled broadly and said, "I have been successful because I know when I'm stupid. I failed when I did not know I was stupid. The key to success is to know when you're stupid and to stick to what you know." When you are operating in your element and performing those duties that make you stand out, it becomes very difficult to micro manage your staff who are equally as competent in their positions.

I have found there are generally four ways to deal with most things. Over the years, I have seen the process outlined below in several different forms using various different words. I am not sure who created this process, but I do know the ideas presented here are not original. However, I have found them to be highly useful when sorting through tasks and placing tasks into priorities, which is why I feel compelled to share them with you.

The 4D Law states:

1. **Do it:** These issues fall well within your range of responsibility and must be addressed by you in a timely and efficient manner. Generally, things that fall in this category are part of your genius, and you are the most capable and competent individual to address them. It is very important to remember to never delay, delete, or delegate any task that falls under your area of personal responsibility. If you consistently fail to execute tasks in this category, it could (and should) cost you your job.

2. **Delay it:** These issues fall within your range of responsibility and should be addressed by you but at a later time. These lower priority tasks need completion but should not displace tasks that command your immediate attention. These tasks are placed on your calendar later and prioritized as tasks that are high

priority for that particular day. Where leaders and managers get themselves into trouble is when they mix up which tasks they should do right now and which tasks they could have delayed until tomorrow or later in the week. Just because you are efficient at getting things done does not mean you are effective and producing results. No one cares if you climbed a latter if it is leaning against the wrong wall.

3.  **Delete it:** These issues do not fall within your range of responsibility and are time wasters. I have had vigorous debates with other consultants and business leaders over the merit and productivity of social networking websites and their function in the workplace. After searching diligently for conclusive data to show that these sorts of websites consistently add value in the form of profits to consulting firms, business leaders, and independent practitioners, I could not find anything more than unsubstantiated opinion. If these sorts of websites produce leads and referrals for your company, I recommend you use them judiciously. If you have not added one contact or lead that could potentially do business with your company, you need to delete this sort of activity from your productive working hours. Tasks best done at home or on personal time need to be deleted from your working hours.

4.  **Delegate it:** These issues do not fall within your range of personal responsibility or within your competence and are best addressed by someone more appropriately suited to handle them. Let me say here that there is a big difference between delegation and dereliction. If you delegate tasks that fall within your competency and/or require your attention, you are guilty of dereliction and are on the sure path to the unemployment line. Lazy leaders cause problems for a multitude of different people within the organization. Companies that do not discipline or dismiss leaders who are lazy always

become bloated because additional staff are required to accomplish the missed or delegated duties.

Earlier, I discussed the principle of knowing when you are stupid. Delegate everything that falls into the areas where you are stupid. For example, marketing is an area where I am stupid. I always delegate those tasks to professionals who are highly skilled.

Another set of tasks that you should delegate are tasks that the company has to accomplish, but not necessarily by you. Forget the maxim that says if you want something done right you have to do it yourself. The higher the stakes, the more clearly you have to see your priorities and determine what and who demands your attention.

# RESOURCES

Resourcing problems are probably the most common root cause of failed projects, failed business ventures, and failed relationships. The resource battle is one your organization will fight at every step of your journey. Proper resourcing is the lifeblood of just about every sort of venture one could imagine. Even the ancient biblical text *Ecclesiastes* offers the idea that money answers all things (Eccl. 10:19). Literally, the ancient text reads, "Money talks." No amount of rhetoric or motivational meetings can foster organizational buy-in like proper funding. When managers and leaders have the responsibility and the authority to execute a set of goals and objectives yet see the initiative is underfunded or completely unfunded, they will not rally to complete the work. Nothing speaks louder to an organization than upper management putting their money where their mouth is. Remember, talk is cheap because the supply is always greater than the demand.

## *Human Assets and Management*

Before we approach the subject of financial funding, we need to talk a bit about human assets and proper deployment. Human assets are absolutely essential to the success of any organization. The idea that your people make all of the difference is not just a cheap cliché to make employees feel important; it is the truth. The products do not make themselves. The orders do not write themselves. The services do not sell themselves. The organization does not lead itself. The building does not clean itself. The projects do not execute themselves. All of these things take people who are committed to doing an excellent job and adding value to the whole. The value of your human asset element is directly proportional to the competency and personal initiative of your personnel. You cannot win the derby on a donkey. I constantly see companies trying to do the equivalent of running the derby on a donkey and wonder why they finish in the back of the pack every time. If you plan to keep running the derby on a donkey, your competitors will beat your *ass* every time.

Team building is a skill you cannot be without in today's competitive marketplace. It is very difficult (though not impossible) to make the leap from a small or medium sized business to a global organization without converting your management processes from a centralized-hierarchal structure to a structure that supports working teams. The speed at which information and markets move in the modern economy make older management models unwieldy and unresponsive. This is the reason many of the world's Fortune 500 companies are team driven. Below we will look at some of the general guiding principles involved in building teams. The specifics of this management model are beyond the scope of our conversation in this book but should be of great importance for further study.

The first step to building a team is to identify the team members required to fulfill the business demands and tasks. It is up to the leading manager or the project manager to identify these individuals during the planning phase of the initiative. The very best place to find team members is internally. No one knows your organization better than the people who already work for your company. These people are already a part of the culture and have probably been involved in past projects or past victories. These experiences can become invaluable to the success of a project. Past successes and exposure to the corporate culture are intangibles that make these types of quality people indispensable. During the teambuilding phase, it is beneficial to research the résumés of potential team members to ascertain their skill sets and capacity to contribute to the overall success of the project or initiative. This habit is especially helpful if senior management has dictated your team includes a certain person or people who you would not have otherwise included. Getting to know the professional background of these individuals will help you understand their perspectives and anticipate the positions and contributions they will offer in the future.

The other way to build a team is through recruitment. This is especially helpful if you "have a donkey in the derby." Often companies face goals and objectives that are required for the company to make the leap to the next level, but they lack the specific experience and skill sets to facilitate that sort of move. This is where consultants and industry professionals can be of great help. For example, if your company has just passed a green initiative and is funding a project to secure ISO 14000 certification, it would be wise for you to hire team members who have experience with and a track record of success completing these types of projects. The same goes for installing any sort of ISO initiatives, a new marketing initiative that includes a market larger than your company has experience navigating, process improvement initiatives, or a whole host of other projects to improve company performance.

During the assembly of the team, it is time to specifically outline the roles of each team member. Working in teams means that you have to have team players. There is no room for superstars or divas in a team, and there should be no tolerance for blatantly disruptive personalities. There is a big difference between strong personalities and people who are disruptive. The actions of individuals who cross the line of professionalism should be indicators that it is time to let these people go. Once the assembly of the team is complete and you have defined the roles, it is important to provide training in areas where the team is deficient or weak. In the very least, you should provide training to make people aware of the general responsibilities, authorities, roles, and processes of the other team members.

## Financial Assets and Management

Financial assets include goods, services, equipment, and all of the tangibles required to complete or facilitate the project or initiative. Asking what, when, and how much is the first step in laying the financial assets plan. The commission of a needs analysis to identify what each department in the organization requires to accomplish the tasking in the corporate strategic plan should be the next task you complete. In addition, a cost/benefit analysis should be commissioned to determine whether the project or initiative is even worth the effort and cost of completion. The reason you would not build a house worth less than your cost to build it is the same reason you would not fund a project or initiative that does not return substantial benefit to the organization. Performing a thorough due diligence is an absolute must before any funding is provided for any projects. It is better to spend $25,000 to ascertain the feasibility of a project than to invest $15 million and find out when the project fails. Before I execute any investment decisions, I ask three basic questions:

1. What and how much is required to walk in the front door of this investment?
2. What and how much is required to maintain this investment once I own it?
3. What and how much is required to walk out the back door of the investment if it catches on fire and burns to the ground?

Almost every small- to medium-sized business I have worked with over the years has been deficient in this area. By needs analysis I do not mean a manager sends a request that reads, *"I needs more staff."* That is not due diligence or needs analysis. Needs analysis requires the manager to justify placing a new financial or human resource demand on the company. Additionally, the manager must provide quantifiable data as to the cost and benefit of the request and whether the need is urgent, what makes it urgent, and possible solutions to eliminate the need through improved process efficiency, feasibility, and alternatives. The other side of this equation demands that the company resource justified requests immediately so the project or initiative remains on track and on budget. As mentioned before, under-resourcing and financial mismanagement are probably the largest reasons for organizational failure. You cannot afford to mismanage this function of your business; it could cost your business millions of dollars.

Cost management during the process of the project is another huge piece of the resourcing puzzle. Every year companies create billions of dollars of waste due to cost overruns resulting from poor cost management; keeping the project or initiative on budget means *keeping the damn project on budget*. This is not a cliché you toss around at meetings that your managers or directors can dismiss later. If your company resourced a project, the manager or director has to keep it on budget. Period. If you resourced an initiative within your company, you must hold the manager accountable to produce results and to keep the initiative on track financially. As the leader, you must set the tone and clearly communicate the idea that initiatives that are over budget, unproductive, or miss deadlines will be defunded, or you will replace the managers. Cost overruns kill the viability and profitability of companies all of the time.

## CONCLUDING THOUGHTS

You need to give your mangers and leaders three specific things to be empowered for success:
1. Responsibility
2. Authority
3. Resources

If any one of these components is missing, the leader or manager will fail. A leader tasked with the responsibility to lead an initiative will find that it does not matter whether the initiative is resourced properly if his authority to manage the project is withheld or usurped. This situation occurs all of the time in companies all over the world and always to the same conclusion: *burn-out, flame-out, or blow-out.* A very dangerous situation results when an individual has the authority and resources to lead an initiative but not the responsibility to see it through to completion. Authority without responsibility usually breeds tyranny and dictatorship because there is no element of accountability present. This is not a trail you want to lead your company down; it will destroy your organizational culture. Finally, a project will never leave the launch pad when it is led by a manager who has the proper authority but has no resources to execute it. As simple as this seems, otherwise competent and intelligent leaders underfund projects all of the time. It is the responsibility of senior leadership to properly fund projects.

The third company I ran was a building services company owned by a gritty Vietnam veteran with a gutsy style and a hard edge to him. I learned more from him about life and leadership up until the point I joined the United States Navy a few years later. I can remember completing jobs on budget and on time, and he would tell me it was because we had the "magic." There were projects we worked on that either failed or became unprofitable, and he always pinpointed the reason as "missing the magic." The magic of leadership happens when you have proper responsibilities, proper authorities, and proper resources. I am thankful for those lessons he taught me those many years ago, and I felt compelled to share his lesson of leadership magic with you. Doing the right things right, at the right time, and for the right reasons is always magical.

# PRINCIPLE 9: BENCH STRENGTH – GOING DEEP

*You put together the best team that you can with the players you've got, and replace those who aren't good enough.*

- Robert Crandell

Bench strength is how strong talent-wise your players who sit on the bench are when the star players are on the field. We have all seen the results of a situation where a player who is less than talented enough to deliver the performance to win the game replaces a star player who has been knocked out of a game due to injury. Occasionally a situation arises where the player who comes off the bench to replace the star player brings the same amount of talent and ability that the star player has to win when it counts. This is an example of bench strength. During the 2008 National Football League season, the starting quarterback for the New England Patriots, future Hall-of-Famer, Tom Brady suffered a season ending knee injury, knocking him out of the game. His replacement was a man named Matt Cassel who had *not actually started a football game since high school*. In fact, he had spent his entire college experience on the bench behind two Heisman Trophy winning quarterbacks at the University of Southern California. When the Patriots drafted him in 2005, they placed Cassel on the roster behind a three-time Super Bowl winning quarterback and a veteran quarterback with over 20 years of professional football experience in addition to a Heisman Trophy of his own.

Little did anyone know, Matt Cassel would become the starting quarterback for the New England Patriots, a football team many expected to go to the Super Bowl.

After Tom Brady's injury, Matt Cassel came into the game and led the Patriots to a victory over the Kansas City Chiefs. After his stellar performance, the coaching staff had confidence that Matt Cassel could lead the Patriots throughout the season and decided to keep him in the starting position until Tom Brady's rehabilitation was complete and he could return safely. As the season progressed, the Patriots finished the regular season with a winning record of 11 wins and 5 losses and barely missed the playoffs. This is an example of how bench strength can help your team to win when your star players are not in the game.

Many times, I find that companies have "Matt Cassel-like" players on their team unknowingly. Your company may be deeper than you thought. Conversely, you may not be as deep as you thought because you have players who have all the indicators of talent but cannot seem to convert their talents into wins. Knowing this information will provide the opportunity to mitigate a potentially fatal flaw before something goes awry. Doing a hard-nosed and honest appraisal of the human assets your company possesses and placing people into situations where they must maximize their talents reveals and builds the overall bench strength of your team. This appraisal will tell you how far down the road your current team will be able to take your business. It is unfair to your team and a strategic folly to try to lead your organization to a place it does not have the skill-sets or intellectual resources to go or to maintain once it arrives.

Every company has star players, or the go-to people who rarely let you down and usually deliver results when you need them. Most companies, especially start-ups and small business, do not see the need to think about focusing on bench strength when making hiring decisions. I have been down that road myself with my own businesses. Most entrepreneurs are resourceful and look for people who can help them with the heavy lifting. There is more to hiring than simply "getting help." Bench strength determines how *deep* in the organization the vein of talent runs. Unfortunately, most managers look for *breadth of talent* when making hiring decisions when they need to be thinking more about *depth of talent*. This miscalculation is a result of hiring people who seem to have many different competencies and seem to be a "jack-of-all-trades." The problem with this practice is that people who are "jacks-of-all-trades" are generally "masters-of-none."

Today's business environment requires companies to hire people who are specialists. Sure, they may have peripheral talents that translate well into working in a business environment, but their core competency falls into one specific area of expertise. For example, when a company hires me to speak to its group or to help lead a quality initiative, it hires me to do one thing – raise quality in either its people or its systems or both. All of my advertising focuses on this one aspect of the value I bring to the table. My firm, Dark Horse Quality Systems Management, does not do anything except raise the personal quality consciousness of individual people. I do not do dance routines, back-flips, or card tricks. I fix quality and management problems by providing solutions in the form of training products, consulting, and seminars. That is it. I know where my genius lies, and I know where it does not. I have made it a practice of associating myself with highly intelligent and competent individuals who can add bench strength to my team when I need it and add value to my clients in specific ways.

## INTEGRITY IS THE FOUNDATION OF PERSONAL QUALITY

When making hiring decisions or decisions to create strategic relationships with consultants or companies, it is very important to begin building the relationship the same way you would build a 100-story building – digging deep and laying a solid foundation. Healthy relationships must have foundations of integrity. Integrity comes from the Latin adjective *integer*, which means *whole* or *complete*. Another good definition of integrity is *consistency*. When looking at people to work with, I look to see whether the person sitting in front of me is consistent with the person whom he has presented himself to be in his resume or portfolio. I ask many different questions and look to see whether he can provide examples of his past work that would be consistent with the presentation he has made to me in person.

Integrity also takes the form of candor. People of integrity own their mistakes, admit when they have made a miscalculation, and bring a solution to fix the error as soon as possible. They do not point fingers at subordinates or teammates. People who possess integrity deflect praise when the team gets a big win and focus the win on the teammates and never upon themselves. They do not take credit for the work of others just to get a leg up in the company or to highlight themselves to their bosses. Their personal lives are lived as candidly as their professional lives. They are modest and know the proper occasion to disclose information about themselves and their work, and they know when not to disclose that information. People of integrity live by the rule that they would never engage in a personal or business transaction that they would not want to broadcast on the evening news or in the morning paper.

People of integrity are of more value to a company than any physical equipment or machinery. They ensure the future of an organization because their personal depth adds to the corporate depth of the company. I have three core values that guide my speaking business each day. During my time in the United States Navy, I espoused myself to the Navy's core values of honor, courage, and commitment. These values act as a lodestar to my business dealings. I adapted the wording of the Navy's core values to one that would provide the tone of what I wanted Dark Horse to project to my clients and to my community, regardless of the number of people I eventually hire. I would like to share the statement with you below:

> **Honor:** We will conduct ourselves in the highest ethical manner in all relationships with clients, suppliers, vendors, peers, superiors, and subordinates. We must be honest and truthful in our dealings with each other and with those outside of our company. We must be willing to make honest recommendations and accept those of junior associates. We must encourage new ideas, be willing to make the hard decisions, and be willing to deliver the bad news, even when it is unpopular. We must abide by an uncompromising code of integrity, taking responsibility for our actions, and keep our word. We will always fulfill or exceed our legal and ethical responsibilities in our public and personal lives

twenty-four hours a day. Illegal or improper behavior or even the appearance of such behavior will not be tolerated. We are accountable for our professional and personal behavior. We will be mindful of the privilege to serve our fellow man regardless of race, religion, creed, preference, or nationality.

**Courage:** We will have the courage to meet the requirements of our profession when it is demanding or otherwise difficult. We will make decisions in the best interest of our company and our clients. We will meet these challenges while adhering to a higher standard of personal conduct and decency. We will be loyal to our company and clients, ensuring the resources entrusted to us are used in an honest, careful, and efficient way. Courage is the value that gives us the moral and mental strength to do what is right, even in the face of personal or professional adversity. We will serve each client with veracity and courage.

**Commitment:** We will maintain professional respect up and down the organization. We will care for the safety and the professional, personal, and spiritual well-being of our people. We will show respect toward all people without regard to race, religion, or gender. We will treat each individual with human dignity. We will be committed to positive change and constant improvement. We will exhibit the highest degree of moral character, technical excellence, quality, and competence in what we have been trained or educated to do. The day-to-day duty of every associate, whether man or women is to work together as a team to improve the quality of our clients, our business, and ourselves individually and collectively. We are committed to leave our clients in a better position than how we found them.

The concept of integrity is at the very bedrock of our society and our global community. Countries that have not espoused this virtue or have abandoned it have little hope of ever achieving or maintaining their status as truly great nations. Any company that sacrifices the good of the client for its own preservation will soon find itself out of business or with minimal market share. This principle is not new, and neither is its application.

In the 4th century BCE, the great Greek historian Thucydides wrote his work, *History of the Peloponnesian War.* In Book 2, Thucydides has the great Athenian statesman and orator Pericles say:

> My own opinion is that when the whole state is on the right course it is a better thing for each separate individual than when private interests are satisfied but the state as a whole is going downhill. However well off a man may be in his private life, he will still be involved in the general ruin, if his country is destroyed; whereas, so long as the state itself is secure, individuals have a much greater chance of recovering from their private misfortunes ( 2.60).

What Pericles is saying is the good of the whole ultimately provides for the good of the individual, while the good of the few or the one leaves the many open to ruin. The same principle is true in business. When you demonstrate the integrity to assure the good of your clients as a group, you also assure the good of your individual business. If you sacrifice the good of your clients in the interest of your individual business, you will ultimately find ruin. Integrity is the bedrock of personal quality, success, personal and business relationships, fiscal responsibility, political duty, military service, or any other situation an individual may find him or herself otherwise engaged.

## SOMEWHERE, SOMEONE HAS TO BE COMPETENT

Earlier in this book, we spent an entire chapter on the subject of competence; however, the subject is of such grave importance that I believe competence deserves a bit more attention here in this chapter. Quality assurance provides the accountability that the production system needs to make sure products are being produced and delivered to the client according to the specification requested. If there were no quality control and quality assurance steps integrated into the production system, as a whole the output quality of the products would be uneven and of poor construction. The role of quality checks is an absolute necessity; however, some companies often find themselves in situations of having so many checks that they end up checking and rechecking and rechecking again products or services that have already been verified because they do not trust the manufacturer or the person who produced the work. Somewhere, someone in your company has to be competent and produce quality work. If you have to create several additional steps to your production process because you cannot trust a manufacturer or an employee in your business to produce quality work, it is time to replace the manufacturer or let the employee go his way and replace him. It is as simple as that. Executing this change in suppliers or employees may take courage, but that is why they pay you: to make the hard decisions. These hard decisions will build your bench strength and raise the overall competency of your business.

If the source of a product, regardless of industry, is not competent to produce high quality products, it does not matter what type of quality assurance or quality control measures are in place. The overall quality of your products will be low because somewhere, someone was not competent to do his or her work right the first time. The bedrock of bench strength is competence. While you can utilize training to fill educational holes in the fence, you cannot fix lazy. There should be no one on your bench right now who does not pull his or her own weight. Incompetence due to laziness should be a sin punishable by dismissal because it not only affects the completion of work, but it also affects your clients and the rest of your staff. These types of people affect everyone and everything in your business. Do you, your staff, and your clients a favor – make it clear that poor performance is unacceptable, make no exception for its occurrence, and get rid of consistently poor performers.

## BUILDING THE RIGHT TEAM

You should not defer the building of the right team to the Human Resources Department of your business. It is the responsibility of the senior leadership and the hiring managers to consider only competent and talented specialists for the position under consideration. This may seem elementary, but many companies hire people who are outside of their specialty or who have no specialty and thus cannot meet the demands of the business and add value to the team. There was a time in business when generalists were preferred for positions of leadership at or above the Vice President level because of their ability to see the big picture and understand how all of the moving parts of the corporate machine worked. While I will admit this is an absolutely essential skill, it is my opinion that the age of the generalist has passed because as our global economy leans more and more toward technology and efficiency, the role of generalists has given way to a new breed of executive: the specialist-generalist hybrid. The reason for this is simple – companies as a whole have become more specialized than ever before. In addition to the specialization of businesses, investors demand that companies be well managed and profitable. They know the leaner the business, the lower the potential cost is likely to be. Investors are also well aware that lean businesses often produce higher potential returns. All of these expectations are forcing companies to find people who are specialist-generalist hybrids to fill their benches.

In the course of hiring, it is very important to hire as many highly talented and competent people as you can justifiably afford. The level of competency you need to seek afterward should be in direct relation to the overall strategy and goals of the organization. Excellent organizations require world-class talent. Your company may not be considered world-class at this moment, and that is fine, but be aware of where your company is on the global playing field and what type of people are require to take your business to the next level. Hire only the talent who can take you there. Whatever your goals, you need to make sure the players on the field possess the right talent and commitment level to get the job done right. Better people should always produce better output; it is as simple as that.

Over the years, what happens to many companies is they hire and promote people who will one day hold top positions in their company but lack the skill-sets to fulfill the demands of the business. This produces a gap in their bench strength. Companies are forced to get these executives ready for these top leadership positions in shorter periods of time because the pace of business is so fast in our global economy. I recently heard a guest on a financial news channel describe the challenge as having to "collapse time." The training cycle of 10 to 15 years ago may have been six to seven years of grooming while the current demands in the marketplace require a company to groom an executive for top leadership positions in three or four years, sometimes even faster. These demands require companies to be very discerning and judicious with whom they decide to promote and invest a tremendous amount of resources into.

Early and often, your business must identify people who fit the profile of the strategically placed leader you will need in the future. These people should be identified and actively developed. The development process of future leaders should include opportunities and challenges that will force the executive to become deeper in his or her own specialty and foster a broader understanding of your specific company and how his or her role interfaces with the rest of the organization.

Many businesses have hardwired growth processes into their executive development plans. Others take a more fluid approach. The approach that is appropriate for your business will depend entirely upon the culture of your organization. Too, this is not an either/or proposition. You may find a blended approach that puts candidates into a formal training pipeline yet allows them the latitude to progress at their own pace. What is fundamental to any approach you take to building bench strength is a demonstration of the candidate's commitment to excellence and employment of the Quality Paradigm in everything he or she does. "Good enough" can never be "good enough." *Excellence* is the only "good enough" these candidates can embrace. The process should also have an inherent level of sacrifice attached to it. This forces the candidate to demonstrate commitment to his or her job and to the organization.

## IDENTIFYING AND MAXIMIZING CANDIDATES

Knowing who is going to be a good fit for senior positions in the future is an important element of developing and maintaining bench strength. This principle is fundamental to giving your business the best chance of survival in a competitive marketplace. A tool that I borrowed from root cause analysis and that has worked very well is called DRIVE Analysis. This process is a simple but effective way to assess and address issues of quality. In relation to building bench strength, I have tweaked the meanings of the original DRIVE Analysis to better fit this exercise. As mentioned before, the candidate must demonstrate an unflinching commitment to the organization; they must have DRIVE:

## D – Define what skill-sets, intangible assets, and interpersonal skills are required to fulfill future opportunities and challenges.

There is an old adage I am sure you have heard that says, *"If you don't know what you're looking for, you won't know it when you've found it."* This simple, old-fashioned common sense serves as the foundation for your DRIVE process. This is a questioning and contemplation phase. There must be a plan set in place so that the candidate has a track to run on when he or she is selected to be a candidate for senior leadership assignments. Generally, there are two ways to accomplish this: planning according to the individual or planning according to the role. The method most appropriate for your culture should be utilized exclusively to avoid confusion and accusations of favoritism between candidates.

Some questions to ask in the "Define" stage include:

- What specialties (depth of understanding) will the candidate need to have?
- What broad general understanding will he or she need to have about business? Your company and culture? The global market? Your competitors?
- What business skills and experiences (reading and managing P&L's, international assignments, rebuilding, mergers and acquisitions, etc.) will the candidate need?
- What challenges will the candidate have to encounter and successfully negotiate in order to be a successful candidate? (This is a "gut check" – I highly recommend finding out a person's mettle BEFORE he or she is in a crisis situation.)
- In general terms, what strengths are required and weaknesses are permissible in a candidate? What

opportunities are currently available for the candidate to mature, and what threats are present that would prohibit the candidate's growth?

## R – Review the talent pool your organization has available.

When sifting through the talent pool of your organization, it is important to remember that you are not looking for talent. You are looking for the *right talent*. There is a big difference. Resist the urge to promote based on talent alone. Another important idea to keep in mind is not limiting your review of the talent pool to the resumes you have on file. Promoting someone into a senior leadership position is a very important decision. Take the time to sit down and talk to the potential candidate. Get to know him or her beyond the black and white resume you have on file. Even if you feel you know these people fairly well, take the time to speak with them in the context of this opportunity. There have been times in the past when I have thought a certain person was perfect for a project, but once I had spoken to him/her, I realized I was mistaken, and subsequently, I went in a different direction. An additional benefit to sifting through your talent is the revelation of unseen and untapped talent resources that lie unused year and after in people who are capable of much broader areas of responsibility. Often people are under-employed or have a skill-set they cultivate as a hobby. These peripheral talents can often offer tremendous opportunities to companies, especially small or growing businesses.

## I – Identify candidates, and engage them in a growth process.

We live in a society that does its best to afford equal opportunities to all people. What follows is the tendency to extend the opportunity for senior leadership to everyone who demonstrates positive potential for growth. This is a gross error of judgment. Your company needs to set the tone for the entire organization by implementing formal training of all-hands in quality concepts to help improve the overall productivity and quality of the work being produced. Leadership and advanced leadership should be reserved for those who have been hand-selected to become a candidate for senior leadership. Not everyone has the potential to be a great leader. Even if a person does exhibit leadership qualities, it does not mean he or she would be able to lead effectively in your organization. The definition of a person with potential is a person who has not actually done anything yet. Competence indicates you have accomplishments. Potential means you have the ability to accomplish a certain thing but have not actually done so yet. An individual with potential is nebulas and uncertain concerning future achievements.

Here are some questions you need to ask when identifying candidates and assessing whether their potential will translate into points in the win column:

- What metric do you use to measure potential?
- What does the person have potential to achieve?
- How do you know he or she has this potential? Be specific.
- Does he or she have past wins that indicate he or she may have future wins? What are they, and what are the details?
- Were these wins substantive, or were they cream puffs that got knocked out of the park?
- Does this person merely project competence, or is he or she actually competent?
- How do you know this?
- How is his or her character?
- Does he or she have poor personal habits, such as alcohol abuse, that might interfere with work?
- What type of message does this person project to the community when he or she represents your company?
- Specifically, what are this person's strengths, weaknesses, opportunities, and greatest threats that would prevent him or her from capitalizing on those opportunities?

## *V – Verify their commitment to the company and growth through the process.*

Commitment to the team and to the company is an absolute necessity. Sometimes individuals will be required to make personal sacrifices in their journey towards the top of your organization. Sacrifice is a healthy part of life. It disciplines us and adds value to the work in which we are engaged. When we have skin in the game, we are more likely to see it through to the end. Some people take sacrifice to extremes by allowing their personal relationships with spouses and children to suffer at the hands of making sacrifices for the company. I am NOT advocating anyone make this sort of sacrifice. Nothing is more important to the overall happiness, sense of satisfaction, and life/work balance than having a stable family situation. For those executives who have no family, it is equally important that they focus on keeping themselves centered and balanced in their personal lives. Personal and family balance cannot be sacrificed for work purposes – *ever*.

Conversely, family and personal balance cannot be used as an excuse for a lack of commitment. Often, this is either used as an excuse for being uncommitted and not having the courage to say so or as a crutch to avoid having to deal with stress. Stress is a part of working in business. Stress is a part of life and is a factor we all have to deal with. The key to making the proper amount of personal sacrifice is setting boundaries with your company and with your family and keeping within these boundaries. These boundaries must be principle-based.

For example, I invest a lot of time with my daughters. They are my number one priority until they go to college and begin to live life as well balanced and capable adults. I also invest a lot of time in my business and making sure all of my financial obligations are either covered or funded properly. My daughters understand that I have to work to make sure they have the resources to live in a stable environment. I communicate this to them frequently. Every so often I will include them in something that I working on. They usually light up at the thought of getting to work with me on "important business" that they have been "specially chosen" to help me with (though as my teenage daughter has grown, her enthusiasm to help me has begun to wane). In addition to keeping a tight life/work balance, I take an hour every evening to read and feed my mind. Also, I will take an evening every few weeks to go to my favorite cigar bar and to have a drink and a fine cigar and to think. This is not a social time for me. This is a time for me to enjoy being alone and refocusing myself on the challenges that I currently face and possibly face in the future. After the cigar and drink, I go for a walk in the night air before coming home. I do this to keep myself balanced and to decompress from the stresses of life and work.

When I was in the Navy, I used to volunteer for the jobs no one else wanted to do. If it meant staying late, I did it. If it meant coming in early, I did it. If it meant standing outside on a flight-line in 30 knot winds and rain when it was 34 degrees, I did it (and yes, it was terrible). If it meant going on a deployment when I was scheduled to take leave, I went on deployment. As a result, I made myself a valuable part of the team and was always recommended for early promotion. That is the type of a sacrifice you need to look for in your candidates. Do they take the easy assignments, or do they tackle the hard jobs and risk failure? That sort of commitment shows they have guts. Do they hit deadlines even if it means staying late or coming in early, or do they blow off time frames and work the standard work hours regardless of pressing issues? The more responsibility they are going to be given, the more sacrifices they are going to have to demonstrate. It is as simple as that. Are they fully invested in the process, or are they holding back? The answer to this last question will determine whether the candidate moves on to the next step in the process.

## E – Employ the candidate in his or her new role.

In the QA DRIVE Analysis for root cause analysis, the *E* stands for *Execute*. In our discussion, the *E* stands for *Employ*. This is the same idea, except in a different context. There comes a point when you have to pull the trigger and trust the candidate to captain the ship by himself or herself. If the candidate has made it this far in the process that you are willing to promote him into your senior leadership circle, you should have thoroughly vetted him over a period of several years and be confident he is going to perform admirably. Finding the trust balance is a hard thing, especially in businesses with millions, sometimes billions of dollars at stake. How much control do you exercise over the new executive? How closely is he under the microscope? Is there a need for a microscope?

Problems arise when we find ourselves in the deep weeds of extremes. Too much oversight prevents the executive from truly leading and managing and stunts his or her development and ability (and appetite) to take strategic and well thought out, gutsy risks. Too little oversight and you could end up off the road and into a proverbial tree and not know why until it is too late. Managing new team members is a bit like riding a bicycle – most of it comes by learning balance and developing a feel for what needs to be done and why. I have a hard time believing you can teach intuition. I know some people will disagree with me on this point; however, I have never seen a successful method of teaching this intangible. Sure, you can teach the principles involved with intuition, but knowing with your head and knowing with your heart are two different things entirely. Either intuition comes, or it doesn't. I have met young business people who have a natural feel for the tempo of life and business, and I have met senior business people with decades of experience who have no sense of situational awareness or feel for the tempo of anything. I have also seen the opposite. Intuition is directly tied to professional and emotional maturity. Some people get it, and some people don't.

Supporting your team members is the foundation of creating buy-in. If your newly promoted managers do not buy into your leadership or feel that you do not have their back when things get into a tight spot (and they *always* get into tight spots from time to time), they will leave your company for another company. Always communicate the idea that you have your team members' backs if they get into a jam and follow through with corresponding action. Buy-in is an earned asset, and if you fail to pay the price in this regard, it will hurt your bench strength because people will leave for better companies and better leadership. Disobeying this principle will result in the person you have spent an enormous amount of money training and grooming leaving to go to work for a company, possibly a competitor, with all of the knowledge and experience you have invested. At that point, you may be back to square one or behind the curve on meeting market and business demands.

If you believed a person is worthy of promotion and competent enough to fill the lead role, support him, and leave him alone long enough to do his job.

## THE FOUR MAJOR CHALLENGES TO BUILDING BENCH STRENGTH

### *Lack of Leadership from the Senior Decision Makers*

Everything to do with building the Quality Paradigm begins with the senior leadership. Quality, leadership, strategy, and implementation – all of these are top-down exercises. Building bench strength is no different. It has to be a priority. In many companies, the CEO actually owns the process of developing senior executives, and all of the executives in the program report in regular intervals to the CEO to give updates as to progress. Often CEOs and other senior executives personally mentor or authorize executive coaching for their candidates. This support from the top downward signals to all of the people involved that there is a vested interest in the success of the bench strength program.

Poor execution from senior leaders and middle managers is absolutely unacceptable. Failure to act in the face of a talent gap that will adversely affect the entire organization is inexcusable. Ignoring a problem and hoping it will fix itself is not a good strategy for dealing with anything, much less a challenge as difficult as building bench strength.

### *Lack of Planning*

As I stated earlier in this book, "Piss Poor Planning Produces Piss Poor Performance." There must be an actionable process developed, in place, and functioning to address bench strength. Bench strength should always be in the back of the executive leader's mind. Senior leaders think four or five steps ahead of their current position, and as a result, they are always looking for the proper people to fit into place to facilitate the over-all strategy of the business. You must always be on the lookout for talented people who can help boost your presence in a particular market or shore up areas in your business that are weak.

When you begin thinking about forming a new company, begin your thinking and strategy seven years out and work back to ground-zero. Establish an overall strategy, and place metrics and milestones in the strategy that will facilitate the progress toward achieving your goals. Part of this strategy should always be bench strength because every business needs to have industry experts, highly trained people, and very competent people. At times, this will seem a bit like herding cats, but business is people intensive, and as a result, you have to keep bench strength in the front of your mind.

## Lack of Qualified Talent Inside of the Pool

Sometimes your business will lead you to places you have never been before. New frontiers of business and opportunity will demand you find and cultivate new corporate competencies and find new executives to lead these initiatives. In almost every case I usually advocate a company to look for internal talent and promote people from within to meet challenges; however, there are times when the challenge you face cannot be met effectively by anyone in your current talent pool. Sometimes there is no way to effectively and economically train and cultivate a promising candidate to meet new opportunities and challenges. In these times, it requires you to look outside of the organization to build your bench strength.

Adding new blood to an organization, especially near the top, brings with it both blessing and curse. New talent often brings an enthusiasm and vigor that can be lost in the minutia of doing business day-in and day-out. Often these people provide a natural boost to the productivity and satisfaction of the element they lead. Conversely, the new executive may have the skills and work ethic required to provide results for the company, but he or she may not be a good fit for the culture and inadvertently cause unrest or uneasiness throughout the organization. Be sure to make a good decision when bringing in outside talent because it can damage both the company and the executive you have brought into the fold. If you happen to be the person brought into an organization, get a feel for the culture and reputation of the business *before* you make a firm commitment to come aboard. Ask people around their industry, and research the history of the organization. Interview them in the same way they would interview you. This simple step can save a lot of pain in the future for both parties.

## Turnover

Turnover is expensive. High turnover rates cause enormous overhead, inefficiency, and waste. I used to work with a business that had a rampant turnover problem. One of its senior managers had the habit of hiring a certain number of people with *the intention* of firing at least half of them every 90 days (this was not a sales department). When questioned about the practice, she indicated rather nonchalantly it was how she "weeded out the people who didn't want to be here." In the course of a year, she had let a large percentage of her department go at an expense to the company of over $350,000 in wasted resources, not to mention the internal inefficiency. Her senior leadership never said a word to her about the practice because they saw no issue and as a result gave her permission to continue the action through implied consent.

I share this story with you as an example of something that is absolutely unacceptable to allow in your company. There must always be a long-term, value-added justification to hire an individual. In other words, the person under consideration for hire must have enough work to add value to the organization for the long term. If this criterion is not met, it may be better to use a bit of creativity with the resources you currently have available and reallocate assets or outsource the work to be done on a contract basis.

Additionally, there must always be a reason to dismiss an individual from your business. Letting people go for reasons that are unsubstantial or unsubstantiated only serves to communicate to the other individuals in the same job positions that they are expendable and of little value. Any praise or kudos handed out by the company eventually comes to be seen as skin deep and for reasons of manipulation. People are not blind and deaf to inequity from their leadership or management. Make sure your hiring and paying processes are legal, fair, and justified. If you have to dismiss anyone, make sure you have substantiated reasons for doing so because your decision will bring change to the individual's life as well as the culture of your business or department.

Turnover is part of doing business. It is unavoidable. Things happen, and people leave for one reason or another. No one likes to let people go, especially in the midst of a down economy, personal challenges, or holidays. However, losing good people to other companies is avoidable if you make it worth their time to stay and address issues as that arise. Studies suggest the majority of people do not leave companies for other companies for better money. They leave because there is an unspoken problem between them and the leadership or because they have a general dissatisfaction with the work they perform. These issues are avoidable by:

- Improving hiring processes to better match applicants with the work to be done
- Improving communication between workers and managers and managers and senior leaders
- Providing employees opportunities to showcase other talents they may have outside of their assigned job
- Creating an accepting and warm corporate culture that encourages diversity and openness
- Scheduled training to better equip management and senior leaders on how to better equip their staff and maximize output and satisfaction

Obviously, the points listed above are not silver bullets with the power to fix every problem every time; however, they will help to eliminate many of the problems that cause unnecessary turnover inside of your organization.

## CONCLUDING THOUGHTS

Shortages of qualified and capable senior leadership can cripple or inhibit the growth of any business. Incorporating bench strength processes into the overall corporate strategy is necessary. Your company must have a flow of capable leadership to filter to the top of the organization as the company expands its interests in the marketplace. The marketplace reality facing corporations today is there is a shortage of well-qualified and seasoned leaders to fill positions critical to the corporate strategy. This reality demands that your company account for it lest you become its next victim. In response to this challenge, organizations have begun to see the importance of bench strength and team building processes to address the challenges head-on.

The senior executive of today and of the future will not be the traditional single dimension generalist who understands broad market driven conditions and strategies. What is needed for the

21$^{st}$ century is a hybrid executive who is a specialist-generalist with deep understanding of certain aspects of business, management, or manufacturing and a savvy knowledge of corporate governance and the internal functions and interfaces of his or her business.

For example, over the course of a QA professional's career, his knowledge and understanding of the quality assurance industry will deepen (because there is always something to learn, and no one knows it all) to a point where it may be generally accepted that he is an expert in quality assurance circles. Simultaneously, he may be called upon to take leadership of a manufacturing company whereby he will need to be savvy to all of the functions and cultural imperatives of the business. His depth of QA experience coupled with his strong knowledge of business will make his chances of being a strong leader who directs the business in a profitable direction very good.

This hybrid-type of leader is the future of global commerce because one-dimensional leadership is outdated. The market demands more from its leadership now, and plans for building bench strength are bridging this gap. If your company is going to compete in the global economy, bench strength has to become a Top-5 priority.

# PRINCIPLE 10: STRATEGY

*Management is doing things right. Leadership is doing the right things.*

- Peter Drucker

Thus far, the focus of this book has been on two things: the Quality Paradigm and business practices (tactics) that create atmospheres of quality and excellence within organizations large and small. There are certain ways to approach certain tasks that, after much trial and error, the marketplace has distilled as some of the best practices available to your company. I would be irresponsible to focus an entire book on cultivating the Quality Paradigm, tactical ideas, and getting the process just right and not issue a word of caution to temper any temptation to focus too much on process at the expense of output. There has to be a few words in this book about strategy and the differences between strategy and tactics. Focusing too much on the process and not on the outputs causes the frustrating dilemma of doing all of the steps properly but not getting the results you want. Do not confuse the process with the output. The output is what pays the bills in the end and is why you went into business in the first place. While executing processes properly, you still have to execute the correct strategy in order to get the desired output. Proper execution is only helpful when you are first doing the right things. That may sound simple, but you would be amazed at how many very capable leaders and managers often overlook this simple idea or have the idea confused and suffer dire consequences as a result.

While there are countless ways to determine a strategy for your business (or your life), all of them boil down to two distinct methods: statistical analysis (data driven, logical) and intuitive analysis (experience driven, heart). Both have their advantages and their disadvantages. This chapter will not attempt to advocate one above the other except to say that you must choose the method that most represents your company's culture, experiences, and approach to doing business. Personally, I like to use a blend of the two processes. I think this goes back to my deeply rooted belief in the Reagan wisdom of *"trust, but verify."* I trust my heart about businesses of which I know the landscape, but I still want to verify my intuition is correct just in case conditions have changed without being aware of it. Sometimes emotions can lie to you, and in a like manner, sometimes your years of experience can work against you when dealing with unfamiliar territory. Additionally, sometimes statistics fail to reveal opportunities only readily seen through the lens of experience. Numbers alone can create illusions of opportunity or threat that simply do not exist in reality. When considering investments or strategy, I always trust my intuition and then verify it with the numbers. Education is the key to making both intuitive and logical decisions. If the numbers do not add up or justify my gut feeling, I take a long look at the investment, and if I still desire to move forward, I do it slowly, with great thoroughness and intention.

Jack Welch of GE said, "In real life, strategy is actually straightforward. You pick a general direction and implement like hell." That seems simple, and it is simple as long as you resist the urge to over-think the process. When I am coaching or training people, I always tell them to do *something*, even if it is wrong. I cannot help you fix what you are not doing, and you cannot change practices you are not executing. For example, in the game of golf, success and failure largely revolve around how you swing your golf club. The magic is in the swing. However, if you are not swinging the club, you are not hitting the ball, and if you are not hitting the ball, you are not playing the game. The same is true in business. You have to pick a direction and swing your club. We can fix your swing if it is ugly, but we cannot fix what you fail to do. If you fail to swing your club in business, you are not really in business. You are in dreamland. Do not be seduced into being satisfied merely with the idea of being in business.

I hate it when people who are attempting to display humility say something like, "It is an honor just to be in the big game. I'm not focusing on winning or losing. I'm just glad to be here." *Bullshit*. Nobody plays in the big game just to be able to say they played in the big game. People play in the big game because they want to be the best and because they relish the opportunity to leave every ounce of talent and energy they possess on the field and prove that they are indeed the best. Moreover, if they lose, at least they can walk off the field knowing they gave their all. It is not an honor merely playing the game. Anybody can do that. It is an honor to be the best and to win. It is an honor to outcompete your competition. It is an honor to hold a party for your company and reward them for all of their hard work in making your company the best damn supplier of widgets in your market. It is an honor to give your all and fight like hell for what you want. Even if you come up short, it was an honor to fight like a warrior. If you are looking to be seduced, be seduced by actually being in business, beating the competition, *and making money*. If you want to play the game, you have to swing the club. You have to hit the ball.

## SWINGING THE CLUB

When it comes to swinging the club in business and finding your strategy, you need to decide what it is you desire to accomplish. What is the reason you are in business? What are you going to produce for the public? Earlier in this book, we dealt with the idea of becoming crystal-clear as to why you are in business and what it is that you intend to produce in exchange for your customer's money. The reason we keep going over this principle is that this idea is paramount to every level of success or failure in your life and in your business. You have to have this idea burned into your thinking. At the end of the day, you have to know your purpose in business and in life. Additionally, this purpose must have focus to be effective. There is no way to be all things to all people at any level of life – professionally, personally, or otherwise. Trying to do so is a fool's errand and the recipe for disastrous mediocrity. In order to swing the club effectively, there are two things you need to do in the process:

## Determine the specific need you are seeking to meet.

*The moment you aim for results, you are in the realm of strategy.*

- Robert Greene

We have already stressed the importance of knowing what you want, why you want it, and the power of focus throughout this entire book. As discussed in this chapter, this also serves as your bedrock for determining and implementing your strategy. Focused effort and knowing what you want affects everything, which is why I have placed so much emphasis on the idea. If you have not bought into the importance of knowing what you want by this point in the book, there is really nothing the balance of ideas in this book can teach you. Knowing what you want is the linchpin to success.

Later in this chapter, we will discuss the importance of not seeking to provide something that is already readily available through your competitor at a better price and at a higher quality. If you have no way of capturing any market advantage (high ground), it is best to refocus your efforts in areas of the marketplace landscape where you are more competitive and to establish yourself as the provider of choice by leveraging your advantage against your competition.

## Determine the conditions of the marketplace and the context of those conditions.

*Those skilled in war can make themselves invincible. Know the weather and know the ground, and your victory will be complete.*

- Sun Tzu, *The Art of War*

What is the marketplace landscape? Where do your competitors sit within the landscape? Does the landscape normally look like this, or is it in the middle of a drought or period of abundance? What opportunities do these conditions create, and do you have the position and resources in the market to capitalize on them? What potential hazards do these conditions create, and do you have any exposure to these hazards? How would it affect your company if your competitors were to exploit your exposure to these hazards? What exposures does your competition have, and how would it affect them if you were to exploit their exposure to these hazards?

These questions deal with market conditions and the behaviors and preferences of your potential clients. Learn everything you can about your customers, their needs, their frustrations, their fears, their desires, and their overall behavior, and then sell them what they are buying. It does not matter what you want to sell people. You need to sell customers what they are buying. *Always* (as in, *always*) listen to the voice of the customer. What does your customer want? If your potential customers are buying widgets, you will go broke trying to sell potential customers zigzags no matter how badly you may think they need zigzags more than widgets. You must know what they are buying, why they are buying, how they are buying, and where they are buying. Additionally, you must know who is selling, why they are selling, how they are selling, and where they are selling. Knowing the answers to these questions will help you to identify opportunities your competitors may have missed as well as reveal opportunities to align your company's strengths against your competitor's weaknesses.

## STRATEGY VERSUS TACTICS

One of the biggest downfalls I see in leaders and people in general is their lack of a well thought out strategy to achieve their goals because people often confuse strategy with tactics or simply do not know what each of them is.

Strategy is "what, why, and where." It is the overall plan of attack in fighting the war.

Tactics is "how and when." It is the specific actions taken during the battles to win the war.

Strategy is a specific forest. Tactics is how we cut down the trees, when we cut down the trees, and how we get them to the mill. Strategy is generally long term, and tactics are shorter term and are often carried out daily. Interwove into the fabric of these concepts is the Quality Paradigm in that it determines the degree of competence with which we plan our strategy and the degree of excellence with which we execute our plans tactically. The strategy and tactics may be ingenious but fail due to a lack of commitment to the Quality Paradigm. The execution of strategy and tactics must commence with the utmost commitment to doing the right things right for the right reasons.

The reason this point is so important is that profits for the sake of profits are immoral and wrong. The idea of reaping profits just for the sake of reaping profits is cut from the same clothe as the criminal mentality that brought us crony capitalism and eroded the foundation of global stability. The criminal mentality believes in taking from others and offering little or no benefit in exchange. It is a paradigm and a strategy that does no good for society and even leaves those who employ its practices in a worse condition intellectually and morally (and often financially) than when they started in business. In 1954, Peter Drucker wrote in *The Practice of Management*, "This, by the way, is why the rhetoric of 'profit maximization' and 'profit motive' are not only antisocial. They are immoral." Drucker believed that capitalism was at its best when there was a moral commitment from the organization to the society it served. In the global society that exists today, businesses and entrepreneurs have a moral obligation to do the right thing in the context of the global marketplace. The Quality Paradigm restores this idea into business and by extension into our global society.

## GOING TO WAR

Everyone who owns or manages a business is a strategist by default and wants to win the war with his or her direct competitors and at the other's expense. Your direct competitors are no different. Every day they are looking for better ways to capture market share and gain a competitive advantage over your business. With all of the warfare in the realm of commerce occurring daily, it is easy to lose sight of why you do what you do. Many times, people's focus is so much on the moment that all of the moments end up running together, and they lose sight of their original goal. They end up fighting over markets that are not strategically expedient for their company to thrive. There has to be a reason beyond the money to engage in business warfare. Capturing market share for the sake of capturing market share is not a good strategy or reason for growing your business. The

Quality Paradigm provides the fundamental reason for creating your business strategy: to leave everyone and everything in a better condition than how you first encountered them, whenever possible. However, this is not a strategy – it is a guiding principle for execution. Finding a way to add value to the lives and experiences of your customers will genuinely delight them and keep them coming back for your services.

Exactly how do you do this for your customers? How you go about leaving your customers delighted with your company and in a better condition after doing business with you is very important. This is the stuff of strategy. It is central to your overall success and to crystallizing your strategy and, by extension, your tactical approach.

Here are three rules about going to war that you need to know before you firm up your strategy.

## Rule Number 1: Never fight a war you cannot win.

*The law of successful operations is to avoid the enemy's strength and strike weakness.*

- Sun Tzu, *The Art of War*

Let me be clear when I say that I do not include in this rule those battles in life that regard issues of principle and moral goodness. We should fight regardless of our chances of success in these wars. It is always right to defend the weak and to stand firm upon the principles that constitute our moral character and way of life. Not to fight on behalf of these principles would be an act of cowardice and induce a condition worse than any loss one might suffer. It is better to die for the chance to live free than to do nothing and exist as a slave.

Some wars are necessary. Business and life require that you engage your enemies or your competitors with honor, courage, and commitment to your personal interests and to that of your company. War may require you make a preemptive strike in order to take advantage of situations that can give you the high ground. Other times war may require you to make a defensive stand against an enemy or a competitor who is intent on taking a position of advantage over you. Either way, you must be judicious in deciding whether a battle or a war is necessary and worth the resources required to win. After all, you should never fight a war that you do not intend or have the capacity to win. The highest and best victory is the one that does not require a war but still yields the same benefits of winning. Only fight when you are certain you can come out victorious.

All business is warfare, and if no way to gain any sort of advantage is apparent, it is better to avoid a losing campaign and live to fight another day. Unfortunately, some companies have products or services that they fund and continue to offer even though these products or services have no competitive advantage. They are commodities and readily available often at a higher quality and grade. Many times, these products and services are sacred cows that eat up profit and provide little value to your customers or your business. While it may be uncomfortable, let me encourage you to pull out the machete and make burgers. Yes, doing so may piss some people off within your company, but the benefit to your company and your bottom line will more than make up for the people you have upset, and your customers will thank you for their better experience.

## Rule Number 2: Never fight a war by which you have nothing to gain from winning. Even if you win, you still lose.

We all know people who fight just for the sake fighting. Often these people do not know why they are fighting or over what they are fighting. They simply want to win for winning's sake. The manipulation of people like this is easy because they have a lack of self-control and an insecure disposition. These people want to be right even if it means losing the people and things they value most in life. Being right becomes the focus rather than executing the strategy for achieving their goals. Do not allow yourself to become involved in a situation where you feel insecure enough to argue for the sake of argument and expose everything you have worked hard to gain for the joy of winning a battle. If there is nothing to gain, walk away and let the other person be right, even if they are dead wrong. Who cares if they are wrong or right? If what you are trying to achieve will not be affected, turn your back and walk away.

If your company engages a competitor over a segment of the

marketplace that is of little or no consequence to your overall strategy, let them have it. Do not waste resources capturing a position that has no value. If the benefit does not outweigh the associated costs, do not commit the resources to win the battle. Doing so may get a victory in the win column but net you a loss in the war.

### Rule Number 3: Never fight a war in which you have an unclear definition of what it means to win.

If you are unclear about what it means to win, you will only have the opportunity to lose. You must be clear about the outcomes of the war before you commit resources to the fight.

Defining what it means to win is the product of a well-planned strategy. Strategic planning begins with determining in specific terms what it is you are trying to accomplish in a specific frame of time (does this idea sound familiar yet?). If you cannot explain what the word *win* looks like for your business or your life, then your strategy is too ambiguous and requires more focus. For me, *win* means providing my clients with high-value quality management training and products and as a result leaving them in a better condition than how I first encountered them. It is simple actually. I provide quality management tools that leave my clients in a better position than before we did business together. If I can do that at a profitable rate, I win. If not, I lose. If my client is dissatisfied with his or her experience, I lose that battle. If my products fail to improve his or her condition or position, I lose. However, I make sure I do not engage in business transactions where I do not completely believe at the outset that I can leave a client in a better condition than how I found him or her. Some businesses do not need my services or cannot afford them. That is fine by me. The world economy is very big. Many companies within my target market desire and can afford my expertise. Perhaps yours is one of them.

If you are not clear about the very fundamental idea behind what a *win* looks like, you will not know when you have won. The reason the world keeps score is that the wins count. If you do not know a win when you see one and your competition does, all you have is the opportunity to lose. Your ignorance is going to cause you to under-produce, and you are going to cheat yourself. This is why you must be very clear about what a win looks like.

## SWOT STRATEGIES

In Chapter 6, we discussed SWOT Analysis in relation to your personal strategy as well as your business strategy. I want to very briefly refresh your memory about the highlights of SWOT Analysis and then demonstrate how you can use the SWOT Analysis to create your strategy. As you remember, SWOT stands for strengths, weaknesses, opportunities, and threats. In your analysis, the strengths and weaknesses portion deals with your internal operations, while the opportunities and threats section of the analysis deals with your external environment.

Once a SWOT analysis is thoroughly completed, it becomes the guiding document for constructing your strategic plan. The general rule of thumb is to formulate plans that:

- **Leverage** strengths.
- **Eliminate or minimize exposure** to weaknesses by employing the 4D method described in Chapter 8.
- **Capitalize** upon competitive advantages (opportunities).
- **Avoid** known risks and prepare for the unavoidable or unknowable (threats).

Using this very simple system of constructing a strategic document will provide a profound effect upon your business. Businesses that do not create or adhere to their strategic plan are moments away from catastrophe everyday they go without one or ignore the one that exists. Often these businesses make little or no progress in their market, and profits become flat because they are just "doing business." It is like being in a sailboat in the middle of the vast Pacific Ocean with no charts and telling people you are "just sailing." In either situation, you have no idea where you are going, and what follows is arriving wherever the wind happens to blow. If the winds are favorable, you may get lucky and arrive somewhere nice. If the winds are contrary, you may be lost at sea or even worse, sunk.

# CONCLUDING THOUGHTS

Life rewards action. There is no doubt about that. The type of actions life rewards positively are those that have been properly organized and well thought out. The more you prepare before launching out, the fewer losses you will experience in battle. Corporate warfare is a serious subject. People's jobs and livelihoods are at stake. The investment of your investors and the personal capital you have invested is all at risk. "Winging it" is not an option. You need a strategy. First, you need to identify what strategy is and how it differs from tactics. Strategy is your plan of attack. Tactics are the actions required to execute that plan. Never confuse strategy with tactics.

The warfare we engage in each day has the potential to seduce us into taking our eyes off why we are engaged in battle to the point that the battle becomes the end in itself. This is an error in situational awareness. You must always be conscious of why your present actions matter to the larger picture and greater context of your business or your life. Failure in this area will result in questions regarding disillusionment and wondering why you do what you do each day. This negative and toxic state will sabotage your efforts to succeed.

In order to become a master strategist, I would advise you to study how military leaders conceive and organize plans for the battlefield and learn the art of warfare. Business is warfare. Life is warfare. Everyday battles between competitors for market advantage rage, and if you are unprepared to meet that battle head on, you will become the marketplace's next causality. Obeying the three basic rules for warfare will go a long way in keeping your dreams of success in the marketplace alive:

- Never fight a war you cannot win.
- Never fight wars where there is no potential for gain.
- Never fight a war that has an unclear definition of what it means to win.

Finally, the utilization of the SWOT Analysis as the foundational document for your strategic plan will set you apart from your competition. As your organization becomes larger, most of your competitors will have some form of official strategic plan. This means you will need to utilize more organization of and commitment to your strategic document than ever before. The victory in battle usually goes to the general who out-strategizes his adversary and then executed his strategy with tactical precision.

# CONCLUDING THOUGHTS

There you have it. The Quality Paradigm and the 10 Principles involved in creating the Quality Paradigm within your life and your business. There is nothing more important to any endeavor than beginning with a strong foundation of character, knowing what you want in any given situation, and knowing what to do to capture it. Quality must always come before management and leadership for it is the foundation of both. I hope this book has communicated this idea clearly through each of the principles presented. Quality is for everyone, but it is not easy. Becoming a quality individual takes a special person to work on building a solid character and developing the thinking patterns required to render his or her life a true masterpiece.

Do you have what it takes? If so, how badly do you want it? Do you want to create the life of your dreams bad enough to stop chasing sunsets while facing east and to turn around and chase after everything you have ever wanted? I cannot do that for you. A reading of this book will not do this for you. I cannot come to your business and train and motivate your group every day. At some point you have to do the growing. You have to do the motivating. You have to make better choices and begin to ask better questions. You have to do the leading at your organization. You and your business have to own your own Quality Paradigm. I can only point you in the right direction. That is my aim with this book – to point you in the right direction and give you a push and to make sure you have properly set quality as a priority for management and leadership.

I know full well that you probably did not agree with *everything* contained in this book or my presentation of these concepts.

That is fine. This book is my take on an ever-expansive subject. I want you to think about what you do believe and to know why you believe it. One portion of the book I hope you do agree with is laying a foundation of character. The nine characteristics that comprise the Quality Paradigm are non-negotiable: Honor, Courage, Commitment, Loyalty, Respect, Duty, Sacrifice, Integrity, and Excellence. You must take full responsibility for yourself and for your business; by doing so you will have taken the first step to installing these characteristics into your life. They are your foundations for greatness. Hopefully you became more conscious of the limiting paradigm and how it sabotages every attempt you will ever make to do something great with your life and your business. These two principles are immutable.

As for the rest of the principles, I know they work because they have worked for me, and they have worked for countless other people who have successfully navigated the waters you are trying to cross. Their application may differ from business to business, but the truth that underlies each is timeless. Here is a brief on what to take away from each principle:

- The principles of Total Quality Management and Continuous Improvement have transformed billion dollar organizations and mom-and-pop companies alike. They are a principled approach to managing the flow of business and the strategic plan set in place to beat your competition and make money.

- Creating a dynamic organization that is profitable requires leadership from the leadership. It is impossible to lead a quality organization without first applying the nine characteristics of the Quality Paradigm. Quality must always precede management and leadership. Always.

- Nothing can replace competence. Education cannot. Prior accomplishment cannot. Potential cannot. Competence is the basic ingredient that animates education, accomplishment, and potential and makes them valuable to both the individual and the organization. At some point, you have to do the job, not just know how to do the job.

- Knowing what your scope is and adhering to the objectives involved in accomplishing your project or mission is paramount for moving your company forward. You must have three visions in your mind's eye: macro-scope, microscope, and telescope. The big picture, the little picture, and the long-term game plan. Keep goals SMART, and you are well on your way to getting the right things done right.

- Without responsibility, authority, and resources, it is impossible for anyone to accomplish anything worthwhile. Businesses and senior leaders who do not empower their managers and leaders with these three ingredients are setting their people up to fail and plaguing their entire organization with frustration.

- If you run a donkey in the derby, is it your fault if your ass gets beaten every time. Your company is only as effective and efficient as the people who comprise the whole. An intentional plan must be set in place to cultivate talent that already exists within the organization as well as attract talent to the organization from the outside. Resist the urge to go wide when considering breadth of individual talent, and instead go deep and look for depth of talent. This will ensure that your company will always have competence at the helm when your key players leave or are otherwise not steering the ship.

- It does not matter if you are doing things right if your strategy has you doing the wrong things. Life is about outputs. Outputs are what drive revenue and pays the bills. The Quality Paradigm advocates tactical excellence but also requires sound judgment when plotting the course and deciding which route to take. Business and life are both exercises in warfare. Whether

you like it or not, you are at war for the very existence
of your company's vision and the accomplishment you
hope to capture for your life. Obeying the three rules
of war will help you to decide when to fight, what to
fight for, and what it means to win.

Now comes the part of the book where it is time for you to
take away the true meaning of each of these principles and apply
them. The true revelation of the essence of the Quality Paradigm
is love. Love yourself. Love your family. Love your career. Love
your business. Love your life. Love your fellow citizens, and
always seek to leave each better than how you found them.

# NOTES

Introduction
1. Victor Frankl, *Man's Search For Meaning* (Boston: Beacon Press 1959, 1962, 1984, 1992, 2006)

**Principle 1**
1. Quoted at Department of the Navy, Core Values Charter www.navy.mil/navydata/cno/DON_Core_Values_Charter.pdf
2. Quoted at FM 22-100 US Army Field Manual

   https://rdl.train.army.mil/soldierPortal/atia/adlsc/view/restricted/9502-1/fm/22-100/ch2.htm#2-2

**Principle 2**
1. Tony Robbins, *Awaken the Giant Within* (FreePress: New York 1991), pp. 216 - 218

**Principle 3**
1. Napoleon Hill, *The Law of Success* (Ralston University Press 1928)
2. Quoted at www.time.com/time/magazine/article/0,9171,1050380,00.html, Michael Schuman, Hyundai Revs Up, *Time Magazine*, 18 April 2005
3. Jack Welch, *Winning* (New York: HarperCollins 2005), p. 247.

**Principle 4**
1. Jenny Nolan, Willow Run and the Arsenal of Democracy, *The Detroit News*, 28 January 1997

## Principle 5

1. Alan Weiss, *Million Dollar Consulting* (New York: McGraw-Hill 2003), p. 103
2. Victor Frankl, *Man's Search For Meaning* (Boston: Beacon Press 1959, 1962, 1984, 1992, 2006)
3. Quoted at http://abcnews.go.com/Health/StressCoping/story?id=4667844,
4. Charles Raison, M.D., Can a Positive Mental Attitude Really Help Me Cope With Stress, *ABC News*, 06 February 2008

## Principle 6

1. Quoted at www.livius.org/caa-can/caesar/caesar_t09.html
2. *Merriam-Webster's Collegiate Dictionary* 11th ed. (New York: Merriam-Webster 2003)
3. The Latin term, *"entia non sunt multiplicanda praeter necessitatem* (literally, entities should not be multiplied beyond necessity)", explains Ockham's principle that "a scientific and philosophic rule that entities should not be multiplied unnecessarily which is interpreted as requiring that the simplest of competing theories be preferred to the more complex".
4. Quoted at www.gerryspence.com/index2.html
5. Ridley Scott, *Gladiator* (Red Wagon Entertainment, Dreamworks 2000)

## Principle 7

1. George T. Doran, There's a S.M.A.R.T. way to write management's goals and objectives, *Management Review*, November 1981 Volume 70 Issue 11

## Principle 9

1. Quoted at Department of the Navy, Core Values Charter

   www.navy.mil/navydata/cno/DON_Core_Values_Charter.pdf

2. John Beeson, Building Bench Strength: A Tool Kit For

Executive Development, *Harvard Review*, 15 November 2004

3. Quoted at www.dti.gov.uk/quality/tools

## Principle 10

1. Jack Welch, *Winning* (New York: HarperCollins 2005), p. 165.
2. Robert Greene, *The 33 Strategies of War* (New York: Penguin Books 2006)
3. Peter Drucker, *The Practice of Management* (New York: Harper & Row 1954)

# RESOURCES

**American Management Association Headquarters**
1601 Broadway
New York, NY 10019

www.amanet.org

1+(212) 586-8100

1-877-566-9441 (United States)

International readers should consult the AMA website for local contact information.

**American Society for Quality**
P.O. Box 3005
Milwaukee, WI 53201-3005

www.asq.org

1-800-248-1946 (United States and Canada only)

+1-414-272-8575 (International)

**Dark Horse Quality Systems Management**

www.thequalityparadigm.com

1-800-419-0002

**International Organization for Standardization (ISO)**
1, ch. de la Voie-Creuse,
Case postale 56
CH-1211 Geneva 20, Switzerland

www.iso.org

+41 22 749 01 11 (International)

**Small Business Administration (SBA) – SCORE Program**

1175 Herndon Parkway, Suite 900
Herndon, VA 20170

1-800-634-0245

www.score.org

It is best to consult the SCORE website to find a local office near you and to find many useful resources.

## BOOKS ON QUALITY, MANAGEMENT, LEADERSHIP

*Out of Crisis*, W. Edwards Deming

*Toyota Production System: Beyond Large-Scale Production*, Taiichi Ohno

*Lean Thinking: Banish Waste and Create Wealth in Your Corporation*, James Womack and Daniel Jones

*The Machine that Changed the World*, James Womack

*The Toyota Way*, Jeffrey Liker

*A Study of the Toyota Production System*, Shigeo Shingo

*Juran on Quality by Design*, Joseph Juran

*Quality is Free: The Art of Making Quality Certain*, Philip Crosby

*The Practice of Management*, Peter Drucker

*The Effective Executive: The Definitive Guide to Getting the Right Things Done*, Peter Drucker

*The 48 Laws of Power*, Robert Greene

*The 33 Strategies of War*, Robert Greene

*Art of War*, Sun Tzu

# ABOUT THE AUTHOR

Christopher Gergen is *"the fixer"*. When it is broken or disorganized, people call Chris to fix it. Chris is the person in the room that says what everyone else is thinking but will not say. He is savvy, passionate, direct, candid, sometimes over-the-top and genuinely desires to leave everyone and everything in a better condition than how he first encountered them - whenever possible.

He is an emissary of quality, management, leadership and success. Christopher teaches business and life principles that will work for anyone anywhere who desires to be in business or who has already taken the plunge and wonders what to do next.

As a dynamic speaker and trainer, Chris speaks to groups, associations, and corporations about the Quality Paradigm, quality management and fundamental leadership principles he learned during his honorable service in the United States Navy and his personal business and life experiences. Chris is a cigar aficionado who is an avid reader, an average drummer and considers the beautiful Pacific Northwest, home.